Dear Parents,

Are you aware that students can lose up to 25% of their reading and math skills during the summer vacation break away from academics*? While the freedom away from school during the summer break can be a wonderful time in your child's life, the reality is children will experience summer learning loss if they don't practice the skills they developed during the school year. That is why we created Summer Vacation®, a valuable investment in your child's future. Summer Vacation is a fun, entertaining educational program to help your child review skills learned during the previous school year and prepare them for the challenges of the next.

This 3rd grade activity workbook has been thoroughly reviewed and recommended by an esteemed panel of teachers. It is packed with fun, skills-based activities for every day of the summer. Some of the activities in this book include:

- New chapter story with fun reading comprehension activities
- New progressive project – "Make a Solar System Model"
- New removable math flashcards
- Counting money up to $10.00
- Addition and subtraction of 3-digit numbers
- Identification of fractions
- Usage of math symbols and place value up to 1000s column
- Spelling and punctuation exercises
- Introduction to world geography
- Arts and crafts activities
- Telling time exercises

We suggest that you work with your child as necessary to complete the activities in this workbook. It may be beneficial for your child to pick a certain time each day to work on the activities. This consistency will help make participation a habit, and will provide some quality time that will ultimately assist with their educational development.

We hope you and your child enjoy Summer Vacation®!

*Source: Harris Cooper, professor and chairman of the psychology department at the University of Missouri at Columbia.

Summer Vacation® Teacher Review Panel

Our panel of distinguished educators was instrumental in ensuring that the Summer Vacation® program offers your child maximum educational benefit. This panel provided key ideas and feedback on all aspects of our workbook series. We welcome your feedback.

Please contact us at:
Attn: Summer Vacation, Entertainment Publications, 2125 Butterfield Road, Troy, Michigan 48084
or e-mail us at
summervacation@entertainment.com.

Cathy Cerveny, Baltimore, MD
Maryland Teacher of the Year, 1996
Fifth-grade teacher; Integrated
Language Arts curriculum writer
Served on Maryland's Professional
Standards and Teacher Education Board

Norma Jackson, Keller, TX
Texas Teacher of the Year, 1999
On special assignment as District Writing
Specialist for grades K–5
Second-grade teacher
Summer Activity Writing Specialist

Becky Miller, Mason, OH
Gifted Coordinator for Mason City Schools
Taught elementary grades 3 and 4
Adjunct Professor at
Xavier University

Laurie Sybert, Lake Ozark, MO
Missouri Teacher of the Year, 1999
Second-grade teacher
Elementary Science coordinator
Fulbright Teacher Scholar

Jenlane Gee Matt, Modesto, CA
California Teacher of the Year, 1988
National Teacher of the Year finalist, 1989
Third-grade teacher

Gemma Hoskins, Bel Air, MD
Maryland Teacher of the Year, 1992
Technology Coordinator for school
Former fifth-grade teacher and
elementary teacher specialist

Charles Mercer, Washington, DC
District of Columbia Teacher of the Year, 1999
Worked at NASA's Education Program Office
Elementary Science resource
teacher, PK–6

Denise Johnson, New York, NY
Teacher Center Specialist in Manhattan
Previously taught grades 4–8
Instructor at Brooklyn College

Richard Scott Griffin, Mount Holly, NC
North Carolina Teacher of the Year, 1996
Teaches grades 4-6—all subject areas
Served as Teacher Advisor to State Board
of Education

Rob O'Leary, Sidney, OH
School principal
Former fourth-grade teacher
Fellowship Award recipient from
Wright State University

Bruce Fisher, Arcata, CA
California Teacher of the Year, 1991
Teacher for 23 years at
Fortuna Elementary
Distinguished Teacher in Residence
at Humboldt State University

Getting Ready for Third Grade

In the second grade, your child became a master of basic skills—increasing speaking and reading vocabularies, reading new words, and recognizing familiar words with ease. Your second-grade graduate may be able to:

- apply complex phonetic reading skills.
- read more than 200 commonly used words.
- use correct punctuation when writing sentences.
- correctly spell more complex words.
- write longer stories on a specific theme or idea.
- recognize nouns and verbs in sentences.
- identify synonyms and antonyms.
- write legibly in cursive.
- understand place value for three-digit numbers.
- add and subtract three-digit numbers.
- tell time down to five-minute intervals.
- understand the value of pennies, nickels, dimes, quarters, half-dollars, and dollars.

Grade 3 Skills

As a third grader, your child will begin the transition from *learning to read* to *reading to learn*. Additionally, your child will have the capacity for more abstract thinking and will start making comparisons of learning experiences in the classroom with his or her own life experiences. Third-grade students typically enjoy collecting, organizing, and classifying information. By the end of third grade, your child may be able to:

- write complex sentences, using more varied punctuation and capitalization.
- demonstrate good literal recall when reading to identify main idea, plot, characters, and sequence.
- make inferences and predictions for story outcomes while reading.
- distinguish between fact and opinion.
- use reference materials, such as encyclopedias, atlases, and dictionaries, as source material for writing.
- write paragraphs to include a topic sentence and main ideas supported by details.
- identify patterns and establish and apply the pattern's rule.
- read a map, calendar, or time line to answer questions.
- find the perimeter of a given shape.
- compute multidigit addition and subtraction problems with regrouping.
- multiply numbers to 9 x 9 and solve related division facts.
- use standard and metric units.
- compare and order whole numbers.

How You Can Help

You can help prepare your child for third grade by making this Summer Vacation® workbook a regular part of your daily routine. Be available to listen to your child read the stories, and offer assistance for written activities and the construction of the solar system model. The Summer Vacation workbook is designed to help your child retain the skills that he or she developed in second grade and to prepare him or her for the challenges of third grade.

CANADA

PACIFIC OCEAN

ARCTIC OCEAN

BAFFIN BAY

LABRADOR SEA

ATLANTIC OCEAN

ALASKA

YUKON TERRITORY

Yukon R.

Whitehorse

BRITISH COLUMBIA

Fraser R.

Vancouver Island

Victoria

Vancouver

NORTHWEST TERRITORIES

Mackenzie R.

Great Bear Lake

Great Slave Lake

ALBERTA

Edmonton

Calgary

NUNAVUT

Hudson Bay

Churchill

SASKATCHEWAN

Saskatchewan R.

Moose Jaw

Regina

MANITOBA

Nelson R.

Lake Winnipeg

Winnipeg

UNITED STATES

NEWFOUNDLAND

QUEBEC

St. Lawrence R.

Québec

ONTARIO

Ottawa

Montréal

Toronto

Windsor

St. John's

Charlottetown

PRINCE EDWARD ISLAND

NEW BRUNSWICK

Fredericton

Halifax

NOVA SCOTIA

4

FACTS ABOUT

CANADA

Canada is located in North America. The ten provinces of Canada are British Columbia, Alberta, Saskatchewan, Manitoba, Ontario, Quebec, New Brunswick, Nova Scotia, Newfoundland and Prince Edward Island. Both English and French are spoken in Canada. Hockey is a very popular sport in Canada. Many interesting artifacts can be found in Canada, including totem poles, which are tall wooden carvings that were made by native Canadians. The only Great Lake not bordering Canada is Lake Michigan.

CROSSWORD

401

Across

1. Canada is broken up into ten of these.

2. _____ poles are tall wooden carvings that tell a story.

Down

1. Both English and _____ are spoken in Canada.

2. The only Great Lake that does not border Canada.

3. This is a very popular sport in Canada.

4. The _____ leaf is on Canada's flag.

Make a Model of the Solar System:

Base Ring

Adult supervision is recommended.

Introduction to the Project

During the next 12 weeks, your child will have an opportunity to build a model of the solar system. This project will help your child better understand the solar system as he or she enters third grade. As your child builds the project, he or she will also be introduced to third-grade science and math, will use measurement skills and organizational skills, and will practice following directions.

Adult supervision is recommended for this activity. Ensure that your child's wire measurements are accurate and that he or she safely cuts and handles the wire. It might be necessary for you to bend the wire back and forth to break it or use wire cutters to get the correct size.

Master Materials List

2 foam rings, both $4\frac{1}{2}$" (11.4 cm)

10 foam balls in the following sizes: (2) $1\frac{1}{2}$" (3.8 cm),
  (2) 2" (5.1 cm), (2) $2\frac{1}{2}$" (6.4 cm), (1) 5" (12.7 cm),
  (1) 4" (10.2 cm), (1) 3" (7.6 cm), (1) 1" (2.5 cm)

acrylic (water-based) paint in the following colors:
  red, yellow, orange, blue, purple, brown, white, black

9 pieces of medium-gauge wire in the following
  lengths: $2\frac{1}{2}$" (6.4 cm), 4" (10.2 cm), 7" (17.8 cm),
  8" (20.3 cm), 10" (25.4 cm), $11\frac{1}{2}$" (29.2 cm),
  14" (35.6 cm), 6" (15.2 cm), 5" (12.7 cm)

ruler

craft glue

paintbrush

scissors

old newspapers

play putty or modeling clay

glitter spray paint (make sure it
  can be used on foam)

toothpicks

Materials

4 $\frac{1}{2}$ " (11.4 cm) foam ring
red acrylic (water-based) paint
paintbrush
old newspapers
play putty or modeling clay
toothpick

Our solar system includes the sun and everything that travels around it. Nine planets and their moons constantly *orbit,* or move around, the sun. Scientists think our solar system is more than four billion years old!

Directions

1. Spread old newspapers on a small table. Make sure to cover the whole tabletop.

2. Push a toothpick into the foam ring.

3. Hold the foam ring by the toothpick, and paint the entire ring with red paint.

4. Gently push the toothpick into putty or modeling clay so the ring will dry without touching anything. Place the painted ring on a clean spot on the newspaper.

5. Allow the ring to dry for at least five hours. After the base ring is dry, you might want to secure it to a table with play putty or modeling clay to prevent it from wobbling.

Extension

From Earth, the moon appears to go through *phases,* or changes, throughout the month as it rotates around Earth. We observe these changes because we can see only parts of the moon at different times. Observe the nighttime sky each day after you work on your solar system project. Notice the different size and shape of the moon. In the space below, draw pictures showing the moon's shape each day.

All Aboard the Space Pod

Chapter 1

Luke was on his bedroom floor working on a space puzzle when he heard a noise: Humm—Beep! Humm—Beep!

Addison's voice came through Luke's walkie-talkie. "Luke, stop what you are doing. Come to the old barn," she commanded.

Luke dropped the last puzzle piece and ran to meet his older sister.

Addison was a scientist and an inventor. She was always working on new and exciting inventions. Luke couldn't wait to see what Addison was up to now.

Activity 1

Skill: Reading Comprehension

Answer the following questions on the lines provided.

1. Who is Addison?

_____

2. Why does Luke stop working on his puzzle?

_____

3. How do you think Luke feels when Addison stops his play?

_____

Luke was always amazed when he went into the old barn. Addison had turned the building into her lab. The lab was full of her inventions. Her best invention was a computer named D.I.D.G.E.T.

D.I.D.G.E.T. was small. He was the size of a small book. His face looked like a computer screen. He could fly or float, and he could talk. D.I.D.G.E.T. knew everything and loved to share facts.

Activity 2

Skill: Antonyms

Antonyms are words that mean the opposite of each other. Match the antonyms below.

grin	sunny
float	sink
exciting	frown
rough	boring
cloudy	smooth

FACT vs. *Opinion*

Listed below are statements about the picture on page 11. Circle whether each statement is a fact or an opinion.

1. The Canadian flag is red and white with a maple leaf on it.   **FACT   OPINION**

2. The snow-capped mountains are pretty.   **FACT   OPINION**

3. The three people standing in front of the totem pole are waving.   **FACT   OPINION**

4. The three people standing in front of the totem pole look good together.   **FACT   OPINION**

5. The polar bear is white.   **FACT   OPINION**

Factoid

Canadian natives are famous for totem poles. People carve animal faces one on top of the other into large logs. Each family has their own pole and the different animals on their poles have different meanings. They are used to tell stories about the family who made them.

Safety Tip

Are you prepared for a fire? Make sure that you have smoke detectors in your home and that the batteries are working properly. To ensure the batteries are good, plan to change them whenever you change your clocks for daylight-saving time. Also, make sure your family has an escape route in case of fire. Practice this escape route with your family and make sure everyone is prepared.

Can you find...?

Circle the items hidden in the picture.

Beaker

Microscope

Flask

Addison

D.I.D.G.E.T.

11

Math CODED Messages

C O D E D = Messages

This tower in Toronto is the tallest building in the world at 1,814 ft. (553 meters).

$$\overline{12-6}\ \overline{9+3}$$

$$\overline{20-7}\ \overline{5+5}\ \overline{14-5}\ \overline{11-3}\ \overline{3+1}$$

1 = s	5 = l	9 = w	13 = t
2 = a	6 = c	10 = o	14 = y
3 = k	7 = i	11 = u	
4 = r	8 = e	12 = n	

I feel _____ today because...

_____

_____

_____

_____

_____

_____

_____

_____

_____

_____

MAZE

START

END

Can you get the facts straight? Choose from these words to complete the story! Beware, there are extra words to make it more challenging!

stripes	**explore**	**symbol**	**yelped**
read	**look**	**facts**	**pulled**
green	**fancy**	**country**	**interesting**
island	**used**	**called**	

Good Detective Work

"Please come here, D.I.D.G.E.T. I need your help," said Addison.

"_____ at this mess! We need to put all these flags in
___verb___
the right boxes, but I can't tell what flag goes in what box. Someone

has put the name of the _____ on each flag, but there are
___noun___

no names on the boxes."

"Here's a clue!" beeped D.I.D.G.E.T. "The same person

_____ the boxes to write down _____ about
___verb___   ___noun___

each country. Maybe we can figure it out by reading the clues."

Addison _____ out a big _____ box. "Let's
___verb___   ___adjective___

start with this one. It says this country is north of the United States."

"Most people there speak either English or French," read

D.I.D.G.E.T. "That's _____, people speaking two languages
___adjective___

in one country!"

"Oh, this makes it easy," _____ Addison happily. "The
___verb___

national _____ is a maple leaf." She held up a flag with a
___noun___

big red leaf in its middle and wide red _____ on either
___noun___

edge. "It's Canada!" she said.

NOW TRY THIS! Ask your friends for words to fill in the blanks, then read the new wacky story aloud!

activity

Adult supervision is recommended.

Shoebox Guitar

Directions:

1. Cut a round hole in the lid of the shoebox.

2. Cut a handle from cardboard.

3. Fold the ends of the handle and glue it to the side of the shoebox.

4. Paint the shoebox and handle. Let the project dry.

5. Decorate the shoebox with stickers.

6. Put the lid on the shoebox.

7. Stretch three or four rubber bands over the shoebox.

8. Pluck the rubber bands to make a tune.

9. To change the sound, put a pencil under the rubber bands.

Materials:

shoebox

tempera or acrylic paint

cardboard

stickers

paintbrush

scissors

rubber bands of different widths

non-toxic white glue

FRACTIONS

Color in the correct number of shapes to match each fraction.
Use the color key below:

squares = red   **diamonds = blue**

rectangles = green   **triangles = orange**

$\frac{3}{9}$

$\frac{2}{3}$

$\frac{11}{16}$

$\frac{1}{5}$

$\frac{6}{7}$

Alphabetize

Place the words in alphabetical (a, b, c) order.
Remember, if two words begin with the same
letter, use the second letter to decide the order.

camera	1.
travel	2.
suitcase	3.
passport	4.
pictures	5.
tourist	6.
vacation	7.
souvenirs	8.

MATH

Follow the patterns and fill in the blanks with the correct numbers. The first one has been done for you.

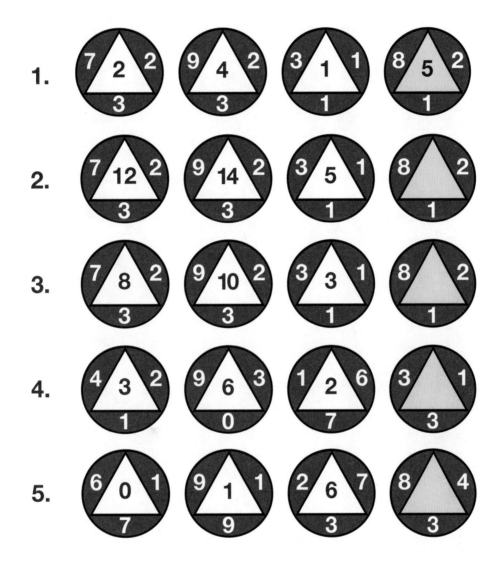

1. 7 **2** 2 / 3   9 **4** 2 / 3   3 **1** 1 / 1   8 **5** 2 / 1

2. 7 **12** 2 / 3   9 **14** 2 / 3   3 **5** 1 / 1   8 ___ 2 / 1

3. 7 **8** 2 / 3   9 **10** 2 / 3   3 **3** 1 / 1   8 ___ 2 / 1

4. 4 **3** 2 / 1   9 **6** 3 / 0   1 **2** 6 / 7   3 ___ 1 / 3

5. 6 **0** 1 / 7   9 **1** 1 / 9   2 **6** 7 / 3   8 ___ 4 / 3

Look at the map on page 4. Describe what you would expect to find in Canada...

_____

_____

_____

_____

_____

GERMANY

DENMARK

NORTH SEA

BALTIC SEA

Hamburg

Elbe R.

Berlin

NETHERLANDS

Bremen

Wolfsburg

POLAND

Cologne

Dresden

BELGIUM

Bonn

Rhine R.

Frankfurt

Black Forest

LUXEMBOURG

CZECH REPUBLIC

FRANCE

Stuttgart

Danube R.

Munich

Freiburg

SWITZERLAND

AUSTRIA

MONDAY

FACTS ABOUT
GERMANY

Germany is located in Europe. Many famous people were born there including Albert Einstein. Germany is famous for its sausage and sauerkraut, which is a dish made from sour cabbage. The story of Hansel and Gretel is a folktale from Germany. There are many rivers in Germany. The Rhine River is the longest. It runs near the Black Forest in southwest Germany.

63

Across

1. A German dish that consists of sour cabbage.

2. Germany's longest river.

3. The story of Hansel and _____ is a German folktale.

Down

1. The _____ Forest is located in southwest Germany.

2. The famous scientist, Albert _____ was born in Ulm, Germany, in 1879.

3. Germany is located in the center of this continent.

The Sun

Make a Model of the Solar System:

Adult supervision is recommended.

Materials

5" (12.7 cm) foam ball
yellow acrylic (water-based) paint
paintbrush
craft glue
old newspapers
scissors
base ring (from previous activity)
play putty or modeling clay
toothpick

> The sun is a huge star in the center of our solar system. It is part of the Milky Way, a giant group of dust, gas, and stars called a *galaxy*. The sun is just one of at least 200 billion stars in the Milky Way galaxy!

Directions

1. Spread old newspapers on a small table. Make sure to cover the whole tabletop.

2. Push a toothpick into the foam ball.

3. Hold the foam ball by the toothpick, and paint the entire ball with yellow paint.

4. Gently push the toothpick into putty or modeling clay so the ball will dry without touching anything. Place the painted ball on a clean spot on the newspaper.

5. Allow the ball to dry for at least five hours.

6. Glue the dried sun model to the base ring.

7. Cut out the sun label below.
   Glue the label to the sun ball.

Sun

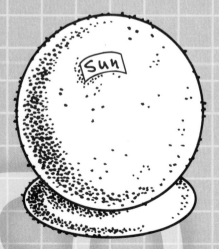

Extension

Astronomy is the study of the universe beyond Earth. Use a dictionary to find as many words as you can that begin with the prefix *astro-*. List the words on the lines below. Work with an adult to determine what the words mean. Write the definition next to each word.

_____

_____

_____

_____

_____

_____

_____

_____

_____

_____

_____

All Aboard the Space Pod

Chapter 2

"I have something really important to share with you," Addison told Luke. She was only in third grade, but some people thought Addison was the smartest kid in the world.

Addison took Luke to one of the old horse stalls. Something huge was hidden under a sheet. She removed the sheet and pushed some buttons. The machine hummed and beeped as it came to life.

"Welcome to the Space Pod," announced Addison. "In minutes we will travel from Earth into outer space to study the planets. In the blink of an eye, we will return with our findings."

The Space Pod's lights blinked. Addison, Luke and D.I.D.G.E.T. climbed aboard.

Activity 1

Skill: Reading Comprehension

Across

1. Addison and Luke will study the _____ during their space travel.

2. Where Luke went to meet Addison.

3. Luke is working on a _____ at the beginning of the story.

4. Addison is in the _____ grade.

Down

1. In the blink of an _____, Addison, Luke, and D.I.D.G.E.T. can return to Earth.

2. (2 words) Addison's invention.

3. Addison hides her invention in an old horse _____.

The door closed. Luke looked around, too amazed to talk. Addison prepared for the trip. She turned on machines and instructed Luke to take a seat. She helped him adjust his seat so that he would have a good view of the window.

D.I.D.G.E.T. tested the Space Pod systems. Lights blinked and buzzers beeped. D.I.D.G.E.T. checked the air and message systems. He checked the Mobile Space Transporter last. This was one of Addison's special systems. It moved the Space Pod so fast that space travel could be done in seconds.

"My testing is complete," D.I.D.G.E.T. announced. "Prepare for takeoff!"

"Buckle up," Addison said with a nervous grin.

Activity 2

Skill: Sequence of Events
Put the events from the story in the correct order.

_____ **1.** Addison tells Luke to buckle up.

_____ **2.** D.I.D.G.E.T. tests the systems.

_____ **3.** Addison prepares for the trip.

_____ **4.** The door closes.

_____ **5.** Testing is complete.

SPELLING QUIZ

Listed below are a group of words that represent things you will find in the picture on page 25. Circle the correct spelling for each word.

1. asembly   assembly
2. worker   werker
3. masheen   machine
4. boxs   boxes
5. tools   toolz
6. robot   robott
7. computar   computer
8. clipboard   clipbored

Factoid

King Ludwig ruled over the German region of Bavaria from 1864 to 1886. He had many beautiful fairy-tale castles built throughout Bavaria during his reign. He spent huge amounts of money to build them and it was because of this that his subjects called him "Mad" King Ludwig. Today, these castles are visited by millions of tourists.

Safety Tip

Do you know what to do if you get lost? Make sure you know your phone number and address. When you go somewhere, like the mall, pick a meeting place such as a fountain or an entrance door. If you get lost, ask someone who works there to help you find your meeting place.

Can you find...?

Circle the items hidden in the picture.

Beaker

 Microscope

Flask

 Addison

 D.I.D.G.E.T.

Math C O D E D Messages

I am a well-known mountain range located in the south of Germany.

$$\overline{9-5} \quad \overline{17-4} \quad \overline{18-4} \quad \overline{10+3} \quad \overline{6+3} \quad \overline{15-5} \quad \overline{22-9} \quad \overline{34-32}$$

$$\overline{8+5} \quad \overline{11-10} \quad \overline{27-12} \quad \overline{14-7}$$

1 = l	5 = g	9 = r	13 = a
2 = n	6 = w	10 = i	14 = v
3 = m	7 = s	11 = t	15 = p
4 = b	8 = e	12 = o	

I feel _____ today because...

_____

_____

_____

_____

_____

_____

_____

_____

MAZE

END

START

Can you get the facts straight? Choose from these words to complete the story! Beware, there are extra words to make it more challenging!

castle	dessert	window	forest	reading
ugly	tales	witch	bringing	reached
house	oven	laughing	pretend	favorite

Just the Right Dessert

Addison was curled up in her _____ seat by her bedroom
adjective

window. In her lap, there was a huge book. Whenever Addison read,

she liked to _____ that her window seat was a time machine.
verb

Today the time machine had taken her to the middle of a great

_____ long, long ago. "What are you _____, Addison?"
noun verb

D.I.D.G.E.T. asked.

"Just a book my pen pal in Germany sent me," Addison replied.
"Did you know that lots of our favorite stories came from Germany?
Cinderella, *Sleeping Beauty* and *Snow White* are all German folk

_____."
noun

Addison turned back to the page in front of her. Today she was

reading about Hansel and Gretel. She had just _____ the part
verb

where Hansel and Gretel find the _____ made of
noun

gingerbread, when her mother called her to dinner.

"Addison! If you hurry you can have part of your _____ first.
noun

I just took the gingerbread out of the _____."
noun

"Now why is that child _____ so?" Addison's mother
verb

wondered.

NOW TRY THIS! Ask your friends for words to fill in the blanks, then read the new wacky story aloud!

activity

Adult supervision is recommended.

Sunflower Magnet

Directions:

1 Draw a sunflower on tagboard and cut it out.

2 Cut the tissue paper into 1-inch (3 cm) squares.

3 Put some glue on a paper plate.

4 Wrap a piece of tissue paper around the end of a pencil.

5 Dip it in glue and then press it onto the tagboard. Remove the pencil.

6 Cover the whole sunflower in this manner and let it dry completely.

7 Glue a magnet strip to the back of the sunflower.

Materials:

tagboard or thin cardboard

tissue paper— yellow, brown

magnet strip

scissors

non-toxic white glue

paper plate

pencil

ADDITION

Find the sums for the equations below.

1. 112
   +211
   _____

2. 305
   +214
   _____

3. 322
   +344
   _____

4. 802
   +101
   _____

5. 461
   +132
   _____

6. 784
   +202
   _____

7. 574
   +325
   _____

8. 291
   +109
   _____

9. 646
   +232
   _____

How many sums are > 600? _____

How many sums are < 600? _____

How many sums are = 600? _____

SUNDAY

Proper Nouns

The days of the week, months, holidays and names of people and places are all proper nouns. Circle the proper nouns in the sentences below. Proper nouns begin with a capital letter.

1. In December, Janet and I visited France.

2. Halloween always comes on October 31.

3. The Colosseum is in Rome, Italy.

4. My brother, Jerry, visited the Taj Mahal in India last year.

MATH

Follow the patterns and fill in the blanks with the correct numbers. The first one has been done for you.

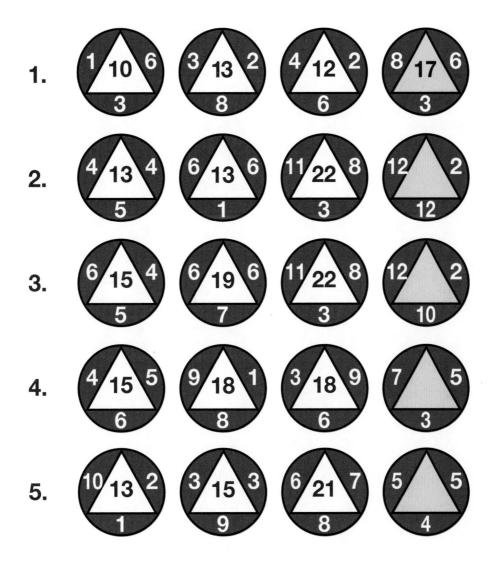

1.

2.

3.

4.

5.

Look at the map on page 18. Describe what you would expect to find in Germany...

_____

_____

_____

_____

_____

GREENLAND

LINCOLN SEA

GREENLAND SEA

BAFFIN BAY

DENMARK STRAIT

DAVIS STRAIT

Qeqertarsuaq
(Godhavn)

Ilulissat

Aasiaat

Sisimiut

Kangerlussuaq

NUUK
(GODTHÅB)

Paamiut

Narsarsuaq

Qaqortoq (Julianehåb)

FACTS ABOUT
GREENLAND

Greenland is the world's largest island. It is located where the Atlantic Ocean and Arctic Ocean meet. Most of Greenland, almost 85 percent, is permanently covered in ice. Icebergs and whales can be found in the surrounding waters. Polar bears and walruses are a few of the animals that live in Greenland.

63

CROSSWORD

401

Across

1. Greenland is surrounded by water on all sides. It is the largest _____ in the world.

2. Giant chunks of ice that float in the ocean.

3. Most of Greenland is freezing cold all year long. Almost 85 percent of the country is permanently covered in _____.

Down

1. Greenland is located where the Atlantic Ocean and the _____ Ocean meet.

2. A large marine mammal found in Greenland that has large tusks.

3. These enormous sea mammals can be found in the oceans surrounding Greenland.

Make a Model of the Solar System: Mercury

Adult supervision is recommended.

Materials

1 ½" (3.8 cm) foam ball
2 ½" (6.4 cm) piece of medium-gauge wire
ruler
white acrylic (water-based) paint
paintbrush
craft glue
scissors
old newspapers
sun model and base ring (from previous activities)
play putty or modeling clay
toothpick

Mercury is the planet closest to our sun—and the hottest! Mercury also has the greatest temperature range of any of the planets in our solar system. The side closest to the sun can get as hot as 800.6 degrees Fahrenheit (427 degrees Celsius). The side opposite the sun gets as cold as -297.4 degrees Fahrenheit (-183 degrees Celsius). The surface of Mercury looks like the moon: It has rocky surfaces, craters and smooth plains. Mercury is smaller than all of the planets except Pluto. It would take three Mercury planets to make one Earth!

Directions

1. Cover a table with newspapers.

2. Push a toothpick into the foam ball.

3. Hold the foam ball by the toothpick, and paint the entire ball with white paint.

4. Gently push the toothpick into putty or modeling clay so the ball will dry without touching anything. Place the painted ball on a clean spot on the newspaper.

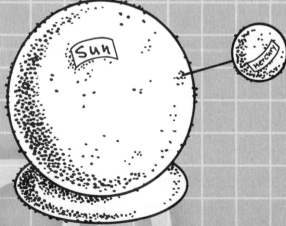

Mercury

5. Let the ball dry for about five hours.

6. Cut out the Mercury label on the previous page. Glue the label to the dried Mercury planet.

7. Measure the wire so that it is $2\frac{1}{2}$" (6.4 cm) long. Have an adult bend and break the wire or use wire cutters to cut the wire to the correct length.

8. Put glue on one end of the wire. Push the wire about $\frac{1}{2}$" (1.3 cm) into the Mercury planet.

9. Put glue on the other end of the wire. About 2" (5.1 cm) up from the sun model's base, push 1" (2.5 cm) of the wire attached to Mercury into the sun model.

Extension

The surface of Mercury is covered with *craters,* or small holes. Some of these craters were made when meteorites hit the surface of the planet. *Meteorites* are small pieces of space material, such as rock and dust. Scientists think that many meteorites come from larger rocky objects called *asteroids.* Using an encyclopedia, a dictionary, or a web site such as **http://kids.msfc.nasa.gov/**, define the following words on the lines below.

atmosphere   meteoroid   meteor

comet   meteor shower

_____

_____

_____

_____

_____

_____

_____

All Aboard the Space Pod

Chapter 3

The Space Pod started to rumble and shake. Addison pushed a button on her control pad. A panel on the barn's roof slid sideways. This left an opening large enough for the Space Pod to go through. Luke grabbed Addison's hand. They closed their eyes and squeezed hands. They were taking off!

When the rumbling and shaking stopped, Addison let go of Luke's hand. They unbuckled their seat belts and moved to the window.

"Where are we?" asked Luke.

"Well, the course I programmed should first take us to the sun," answered Addison.

"Filters are in place," reported D.I.D.G.E.T.

Activity 1

Skill: Vocabulary

Circle the letter of the definition that shows how each of the words below is used in the story.

1. rumble
   a. stand still
   b. fight
   c. roar
   d. dance

2. program
   a. play
   b. force
   c. TV show
   d. instruct

3. squeeze
   a. hold tight
   b. loosely hold
   c. roll
   d. pinch

"What does D.I.D.G.E.T. mean by filters?" asked Luke.

"There are special screens on the window so that we can look at bright things without hurting our eyes," Addison explained.

"Look at that!" Luke pointed to a huge explosion on the sun.

"You are watching a solar flare," said D.I.D.G.E.T. "It is a release of energy in the form of light and heat on the sun's surface."

The sun seemed to fill the entire window. Without a word, Luke and Addison watched the sun disappear from the window as the Space Pod turned in the direction of their first planet.

Activity 2

Skill: Adjectives

Adjectives **are words that describe people, places, and things. Use adjectives to answer the questions below.**

1. List two adjectives you would use to describe a solar flare.

_____

2. What kind of screens are on the windows?

_____

3. The filters allow Addison and Luke to look at what kind of things?

_____

CONTRACTIONS

Contractions are made by combining two words into one. An apostrophe (') is used to stand for the missing letters.

Example: could not = couldn't

I am = I'm

Write the contractions for the words below.

1. do not   __ __ __' __

2. is not   __ __ __' __

3. they are   __ __ __ __' __ __

4. I have   __' __ __

5. we have   __ __' __ __

6. they will   __ __ __ __' __ __

7. we are   __ __' __ __

8. you will   __ __ __' __ __

Factoid

Greenland is one of the least inhabited areas of the world. There are only about 150 towns and villages in all of Greenland. There are no railroads, few roads, and not many cars. People usually travel by plane, helicopter or dog sled.

Safety Tip

Beware of strangers. Make sure you do not go anywhere with someone you do not know. Remember: If someone makes you feel uncomfortable, you can say "No!" and get away from them.

Can you find...?

Circle the items hidden in the picture.

Beaker

Microscope

Flask

Addison

D.I.D.G.E.T.

Math CODED Messages

The two languages spoken in Greenland are:

$\overline{26-18}$ $\overline{9+4}$ $\overline{7+2}$ $\overline{18-9}$ $\overline{23-17}$ $\overline{18-11}$ $\overline{32-31}$ $\overline{5+1}$ $\overline{18-7}$ $\overline{18-13}$ $\overline{2+8}$

and

$\overline{16-5}$ $\overline{1+0}$ $\overline{29-23}$ $\overline{2+3}$ $\overline{19-17}$ $\overline{8+4}$

1 = a	5 = i	9 = e	13 = r
2 = s	6 = n	10 = c	
3 = d	7 = l	11 = d	
4 = b	8 = g	12 = h	

I feel _____ today because…

_____

_____

_____

_____

_____

_____

_____

_____

_____

_____

_____

MAZE

END

START

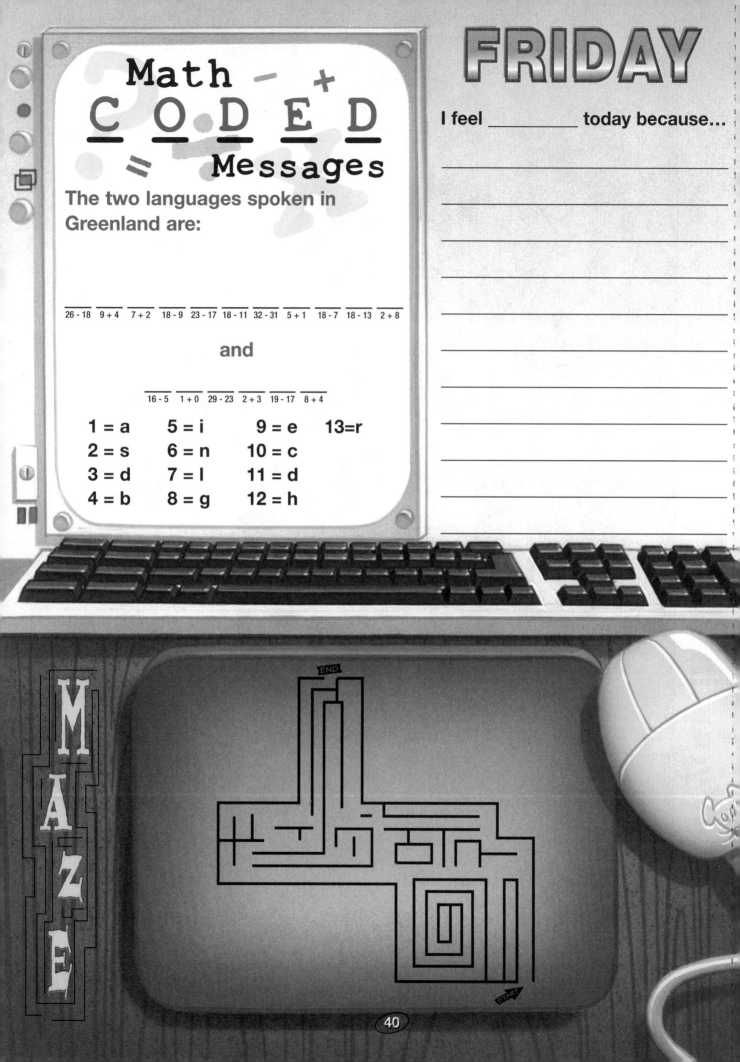

Can you get the facts straight? Choose from these words to complete the story! Beware, there are extra words to make it more challenging!

huge	**information**	**blanket**	**clicked**
climbed	**science**	**hummed**	**jumped**
report	**summer**	**sound**	**called**
reindeer	**replied**	**ice**	**largest**

A Chilly Question

"I need _____, D.I.D.G.E.T.," said Addison. "The science club
_{noun}
has asked me to do a _____ on Greenland. What do we know
_{noun}
about Greenland?"

D.I.D.G.E.T. clicked and _____ as he checked his files. "It's an
_{verb}
island," he printed out.

"Right! It's the world's _____ island. What else?"
_{adjective}
There were more hums and clicks. D.I.D.G.E.T.'s list was long.

"In the _____, Greenland stays light almost all night long.
_{noun}
In the winter, it's dark there almost all day long. That's because it's so
far north."

Addison nodded. "What else?"

"B-b-b-b-eep, b-b-b-b-b-b-b-eep, b-b-b-b-b-b-b-b-b-b-b-b-b-eep!"
said D.I.D.G.E.T. He made the _____ over and over.
_{noun}

"Help, Mother!" _____ Addison. "I think D.I.D.G.E.T. is broken!
_{verb}
His beep is stuck!"

"What did you ask him?" Addison's mother wanted to know.

"Just questions about Greenland," _____ Addison.
_{verb}

"That's it, then," laughed her mother. "He's not stuck, he's shivering!"

Addison went over to look at D.I.D.G.E.T.'s display. "Most of
Greenland is covered by a _____ glacier," she read. "Oh Mother,
_{adjective}
it's covered with _____!"
_{noun}

41

activity

Adult supervision is recommended.

Apple Feeder

Directions:

Materials:

wire hanger

wire cutters

needle-nose pliers

apple

ribbon

1 Have an adult help you use wire cutters to make a cut in the middle of the bottom of the hanger.

2 Bend the hanger into the shape shown.

3 Use needle-nose pliers to twist the ends together tightly.

4 Tie a ribbon on the top of the hanger.

5 Push an apple onto the twisted ends.

6 Hang the hanger in a tree or near a bird feeder. Watch for orioles, robins and tanagers. They all like fruit.

PERIMETER

Perimeter is the distance around a shape. You can find the perimeter by counting the centimeters for each side and adding them together.

Example: 2 + 2 + 2 + 2 = 8

The perimeter is 8 centimeters.

What is the perimeter in centimeters for each shape below?

_____ Centimeters

_____ Centimeters

_____ Centimeters

Long Vowels

Long vowels sound like their name a, e, i, o and u.
Circle the words that use a long vowel.

cat	tub
kite	cube
cake	sheep
wave	ten
note	five
not	lit

MATH

Follow the patterns and fill in the blanks with the correct numbers. The first one has been done for you.

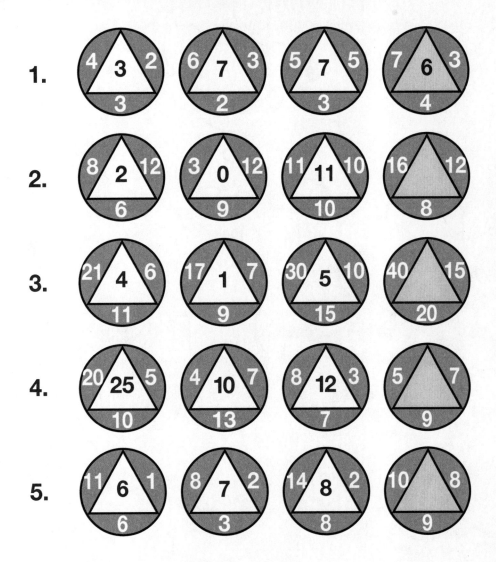

1. 4 3 2 / 3   6 7 3 / 2   5 7 5 / 3   7 6 3 / 4

2. 8 2 12 / 6   3 0 12 / 9   11 11 10 / 10   16 12 / 8

3. 21 4 6 / 11   17 1 7 / 9   30 5 10 / 15   40 15 / 20

4. 20 25 5 / 10   4 10 7 / 13   8 12 3 / 7   5 7 / 9

5. 11 6 1 / 6   8 7 2 / 3   14 8 2 / 8   10 8 / 9

Look at the map on page 32. Describe what you would expect to find in Greenland...

_____

_____

_____

_____

_____

IRELAND

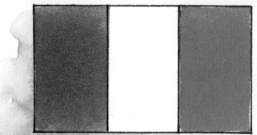

NORTH CHANNEL

ATLANTIC OCEAN

IRISH SEA

Londonderry

Lough Neagh

Belfast

Galway

Shannon River

DUBLIN

Kilkenny

Limerick
Tipperary

Killarney

Waterford

Cork

ST. GEORGE'S CHANNEL

FACTS ABOUT

IRELAND

63

Ireland is located in the western part of Europe. It is bordered by the Atlantic Ocean on three sides, and the Irish Sea on the fourth. The Shannon River is the longest river in Ireland. Ireland is divided into 26 counties. St. Patrick is the patron saint of Ireland. The shamrock is the national emblem. One of the most popular sports in Ireland is rugby.

CROSSWORD

Across

1. A plant with 3 leaves which is the national emblem of Ireland.

2. A popular sport in Ireland. You can kick, throw or carry the ball to the goal.

3. Ireland is bordered by the Atlantic Ocean on three sides and the _____ Sea on the fourth.

Down

1. The _____ River is the longest river in Ireland.

2. St. _____ is the patron saint of Ireland.

3. Ireland is divided into 26 of these.

Make a Model of the Solar System: Venus

Adult supervision is recommended.

Materials

2" (5.1 cm) foam ball
4" (10.2 cm) piece of
    medium-gauge wire
ruler
white acrylic (water-based) paint
brown acrylic (water-based) paint
paintbrush
craft glue
scissors
old newspapers
model from the previous activity
play putty or modeling clay
toothpick

Venus is the second planet from the sun and is next to Earth. Venus is almost exactly the same size as Earth. Its surface is similar to Earth's, except that it has no oceans. The temperature on Venus is much hotter than that on Earth: It gets as hot as 900 degrees Fahrenheit (484 degrees Celsius). Even though Venus is covered with poisonous gas clouds, it looks so bright from the Earth that it is still called the Evening Star.

Directions

1. Spread clean newspapers to cover a table.

2. Push a toothpick into the foam ball.

3. Hold the foam ball by the toothpick, and paint the entire ball with tan paint. To make tan paint, you can mix white paint with a small amount of brown paint.

4. Gently push the toothpick into putty or modeling clay so the ball will dry without touching anything. Place the painted ball on a clean spot on the newspaper.

Venus

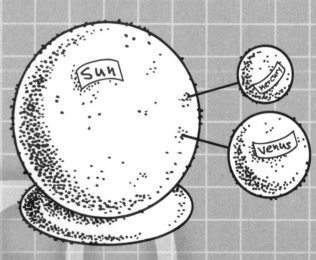

5. Let the ball dry for about five hours.

6. Cut out the Venus label on the previous page. Glue the label to the dried Venus planet.

7. Measure the wire so that it is 4" (10.2 cm) long. Have an adult break or cut the wire to the correct length.

8. Put glue on one end of the wire. Push the wire about $\frac{1}{2}$" (1.3 cm) into the Venus planet model.

9. Put glue on the other end of the wire. About $\frac{3}{4}$" (1.9 cm) from the Mercury wire, push 1" (2.5 cm) of the wire attached to Venus into the sun model.

Extension

More U.S. and Russian spacecraft have visited Venus than have visited any other planet! Imagine that you and your family are invited on a mission to Venus. In the space below, draw the spacecraft you would like to travel in, or write a paragraph about what you think space travel would be like.

All Aboard the Space Pod

Chapter 4

"My very educated mother just served us nine pizzas," Addison chanted as she worked at the computer.

"What are you talking about?" asked Luke.

Addison looked up. "It's how I remember the order of the planets. The first letter of each word matches the first letter of a planet: My—Mercury, very—Venus, educated—Earth, mother—Mars, just—. . ."

"Jupiter! I get it," Luke interrupted. "Now, why are we saying this?"

"I programmed our trip so that we would go to the sun first and then to the planets in this order. Mercury is the planet closest to the sun. This program will tell us where we go next," Addison said.

Activity 1

Skill: Reading Comprehension

On the first line, write Addison's memory sentence. Then write, in order, the names of the planets.

_____

_____

_____

_____

_____

_____

_____

"Where did we stop?" Luke asked. "Mercury, Venus, Earth, Mars, Jupiter. . .Served—Saturn."

"Us—Uranus, nine—Neptune," Addison added.

"Pizzas—Pluto!" they yelled together.

"Speaking of pizzas, I'm hungry," Luke announced.

"When we went to the space museum, I bought ice cream like the astronauts used to eat," Addison said, and handed a bag to Luke.

Luke tasted the bag's contents and made a face. "This doesn't taste like ice cream."

"It's freeze-dried," Addison said. "Most of the water and oxygen have been removed from it. Freeze-dried foods last for years."

"I think I'd rather have pizza," Luke said.

"Next stop, Mercury," said D.I.D.G.E.T.

Activity 2

Skill: Creative Writing

Silly sentences can sometimes help us remember important information. Can you think of another way to remember the order of the planets? Write your silly sentence in the space provided.

_____

_____

_____

_____

RHYMING WORDS

Look at the picture on page 53 and find the items that rhyme with the words below.

1. deep   __ __ __ __ __

2. tomatoes   __ __ __ __ __ __ __ __

3. box   __ __ __

4. luck   __ __ __ __ __

5. tell   __ __ __ __

6. lock   __ __ __ __

7. mouse   __ __ __ __ __

8. tall   __ __ __ __

Factoid

Potatoes have been a staple of the Irish diet for hundreds of years. In the mid 1800s, a plant disease wiped out the potato crop. About one million people died from starvation and another one million left the country.

Safety Tip

Do you know about germs? Washing your hands is a very important part of good manners. Germs on your hands can make you and others sick. It is very important to wash your hands when they are dirty, after using the bathroom, or when you cough, sneeze, or blow your nose.

Can you find...?

Circle the items hidden in the picture.

Beaker

Microscope

Flask

Addison

D.I.D.G.E.T.

Math CODED Messages

Because of the green rolling hills and countryside, Ireland is known as the:

$$\overline{6+6}\ \overline{19-16}\ \overline{11+1}\ \overline{29-15}\ \overline{7+1}\ \overline{19-10}\ \overline{32-21}$$

$$\overline{21-15}\ \overline{30-28}\ \overline{22-13}\ \overline{24-12}$$

1 = p	5 = u	9 = l	13 = t
2 = s	6 = i	10 = g	14 = r
3 = m	7 = y	11 = d	
4 = n	8 = a	12 = e	

I feel _____ today because...

_____

_____

_____

_____

_____

_____

_____

_____

_____

_____

MAZE

END

START

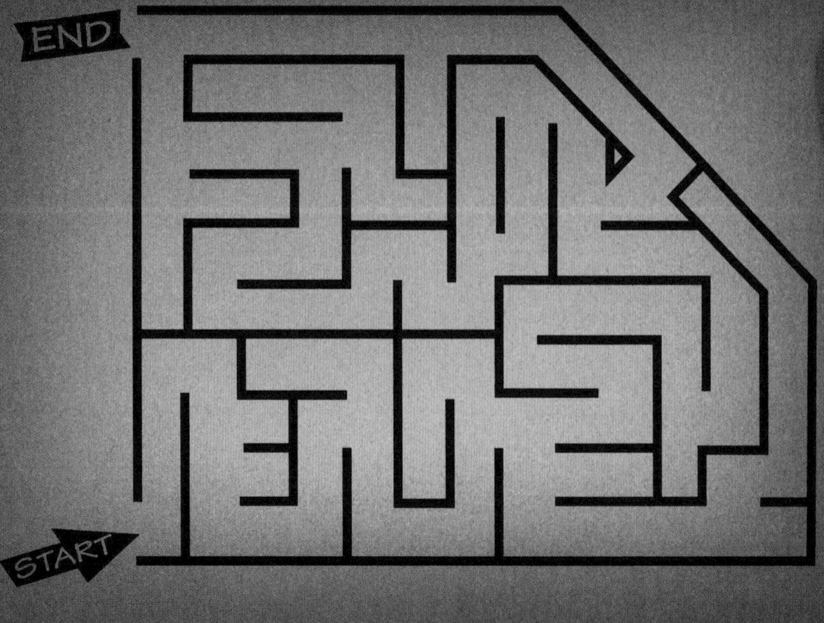

Can you get the facts straight? Choose from these words to complete the story! Beware, there are extra words to make it more challenging!

legs	acrobat	princess	jump
laughed	stone	shamrock	photographs
people	rainy	good	hang
stand	stories	shouted	

The Blarney Stone

D.I.D.G.E.T. was storing pictures. Addison watched carefully to be sure that all the saved _____ were _____ ones. "Stop,
                                           noun   adjective
D.I.D.G.E.T!" she said. "That one's upside down."

Sure enough, D.I.D.G.E.T. was saving a picture of Addison's Uncle Bob—but Uncle Bob's face was at the bottom of the picture and his _____ were at the top. Addison looked closer. That was funny. The
noun
other _____ in the picture were right side up. A man held Uncle
        noun
Bob's legs. Uncle Bob had his hands on iron bars. It looked as if he was trying to _____ upside down on a staircase.
                          verb

"I don't understand," Addison said. "Uncle Bob isn't an _____.
                                                              noun
What is he doing?"

"He's kissing the Blarney Stone," _____ Addison's mother.
                                       verb
"There's a special stone in the wall of Blarney Castle in Ireland.
People say that if you _____ backwards over the castle wall and
                          verb
kiss the _____, you will be able to talk and tell _____ better than
            noun   noun
anybody."

That explained everything. Uncle Bob was the best storyteller that Addison knew!

Ask your friends for words to fill in the blanks, then read the new wacky story aloud!

55

activity

Adult supervision is recommended.

Star Banner

Directions:

1. Glue two pieces of blue construction paper together to make a long banner.

2. Cut white strips of paper and glue them evenly down the length of the banner.

3. Glue two pieces of red construction paper together.

4. Trim one side and one end of the red paper so it makes a banner smaller than the blue banner.

5. Glue the red banner to the center of the blue-striped banner.

6. Draw and cut out three big stars from yellow paper.

7. Overlap and glue them to the red section of the banner.

8. Draw and cut out two more big yellow stars.

9. Punch holes in the banner and the stars. Tie them together as shown.

Materials:

construction paper: red, white, blue, and yellow

scissors

non-toxic white glue

pencil

yarn or string

hole punch

SUBTRACTION

Find the difference for the equations below.

1. $\begin{array}{r} 499 \\ -\ 127 \\ \hline \end{array}$

2. $\begin{array}{r} 652 \\ -\ 241 \\ \hline \end{array}$

3. $\begin{array}{r} 887 \\ -\ 217 \\ \hline \end{array}$

4. $\begin{array}{r} 767 \\ -\ 554 \\ \hline \end{array}$

5. $\begin{array}{r} 980 \\ -\ 480 \\ \hline \end{array}$

6. $\begin{array}{r} 599 \\ -\ \ 99 \\ \hline \end{array}$

7. $\begin{array}{r} 411 \\ -\ 310 \\ \hline \end{array}$

8. $\begin{array}{r} 969 \\ -\ 358 \\ \hline \end{array}$

9. $\begin{array}{r} 893 \\ -\ 342 \\ \hline \end{array}$

How many answers are > 500? _____

How many answers are < 500? _____

How many answers are = 500? _____

Blends

Blends are two consonants put together.

Example: dr-eam, dream

Circle the words below that start with a blend.

sticker   frog

slip   ball

take   grab

look   park

trick

MATH

Follow the patterns and fill in the blanks with the correct numbers. The first one has been done for you.

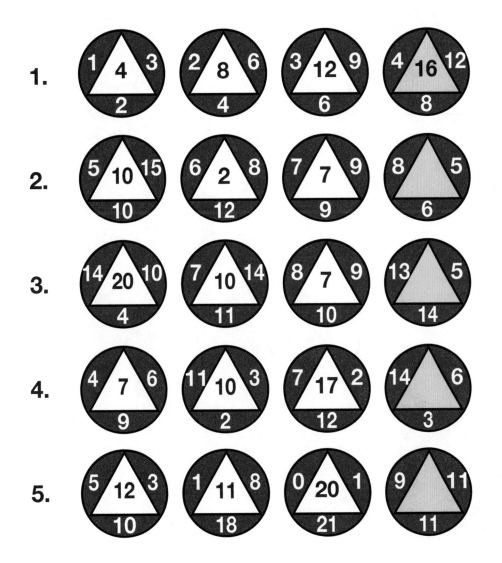

1.
   - 1 **4** 3 / 2
   - 2 **8** 6 / 4
   - 3 **12** 9 / 6
   - 4 **16** 12 / 8

2.
   - 5 **10** 15 / 10
   - 6 **2** 8 / 12
   - 7 **7** 9 / 9
   - 8 5 / 6

3.
   - 14 **20** 10 / 4
   - 7 **10** 14 / 11
   - 8 **7** 9 / 10
   - 13 5 / 14

4.
   - 4 **7** 6 / 9
   - 11 **10** 3 / 2
   - 7 **17** 2 / 12
   - 14 6 / 3

5.
   - 5 **12** 3 / 10
   - 1 **11** 8 / 18
   - 0 **20** 1 / 21
   - 9 11 / 11

Look at the map on page 46. Describe what you would expect to find in Ireland...

_____

_____

_____

_____

_____

SEA OF JAPAN

PACIFIC OCEAN

Sapporo

HOKKAIDŌ

Sendai

HONSHŪ

Kyoto
Kōbe
Hiroshima
Osaka
Nagoya
Mt. Fuji
★ TOKYO
Yokohama
Kawasaki

Nagasaki

SHIKOKU

KYŪSHŪ

JAPAN

FACTS ABOUT

JAPAN

Japan consists of a string of 4,000 islands located off the east coast of Asia in the Pacific Ocean. In Japan, people eat with chopsticks and rice is an important part of their diet. It is a custom to remove your shoes and put on slippers when you enter a house in Japan. May 5th is Children's Day in Japan. The Cherry Blossom is Japan's national flower.

63

CROSSWORD

401

Across

1. In Japan, instead of using forks and knives, people eat with _____.

2. The blossom of this small red fruit is Japan's national flower.

Down

1. In Japan, when people enter a house, they remove their _____ and put on slippers.

2. Japan is made up of about 4,000 islands in the _____ Ocean.

3. This small white grain is an important part of the Japanese diet.

4. Children's Day is a holiday celebrated in Japan on the fifth day of the fifth month of the year, so it is celebrated in this month.

Make a Model of the Solar System: Earth

Adult supervision is recommended.

Materials

2" (5.1 cm) foam ball
5" (12.7 cm) piece of
     medium-gauge wire
ruler
blue acrylic (water-based) paint
paintbrush
craft glue
scissors
old newspapers
model from the previous activity
play putty or modeling clay
toothpick

Earth is our planet. It is the third planet from the sun. Most of the Earth's surface is water. It is called the Big Blue Planet because it looks blue from space. If you were in space, you could also see Earth's brown and green land surfaces and white clouds. The temperatures and gases on Earth make it the only planet you can live on.

Directions

1. Spread clean newspapers on a table.

2. Push a toothpick into the foam ball.

3. Hold the foam ball by the toothpick, and paint the entire ball with blue paint.

4. Gently push the toothpick into putty or modeling clay so the ball will dry without touching anything. Place the painted ball on a clean spot on the newspaper.

5. Let the ball dry for about five hours.

6. Cut out the Earth label below. Glue the label to the dried Earth planet.

Earth

7. Measure the wire so that it is 5" (12.7 cm) long. Have an adult break or cut the wire to the correct length.

8. Put glue on one end of the wire. Push the wire about $\frac{1}{2}$" (1.3 cm) into the Earth planet model.

9. Put glue on the other end of the wire. Push 1" (2.5 cm) of the wire attached to Earth into the sun model about $1\frac{1}{8}$" (2.9 cm) from the Venus wire.

Extension

Have you ever heard of a Moon Tree? As part of *Apollo 14's* mission to the moon in 1971, astronaut Stuart Roosa took seeds from five different kinds of trees with him when he orbited the moon. These seeds were planted and observed after the astronauts returned to Earth. The seedlings grown were handed out and planted during our nation's bicentennial celebrations. People call the trees "Moon Trees" because they grew from seeds that traveled to the moon.

To find more about what kinds of tree seeds went to the moon, look for books at your local library. Draw a picture of the moon and the Moon Trees in the space below.

All Aboard the Space Pod

Chapter 5

Addison wanted to use her new Super Scope to get a better view of Mercury. The Super Scope looked like a telescope, but it was much more powerful. It could even take digital pictures!

As Addison moved to get the Super Scope from the cabinet, her legs flipped up. She was moving, but not walking. She was floating! Luke and Addison had been so excited about watching the activity on the sun that they had not realized that they had floated from their chairs to the window.

They had fun floating for a while and then went back to the window to see Mercury.

Activity 1

Skill: Word Search

Nouns name people, places and things. Find the nouns from the word bank that are hidden in the puzzle. Words can be vertical, horizontal or diagonal.

ADDISON

D.I.D.G.E.T.

MERCURY

SUPERSCOPE

CABINET

EARTH

METEORITE

VENUS

CRATER

LUKE

S	N	Z	V	V	B	L	C	E	S	K	K	N	E	G
S	O	G	B	P	T	W	C	U	C	Q	J	H	A	O
J	S	B	Y	X	W	K	P	P	F	F	N	W	R	O
A	I	X	N	L	F	E	E	T	A	W	F	V	T	I
O	D	S	Y	R	R	T	P	D	Q	L	D	N	H	V
V	D	F	X	S	H	J	K	I	J	F	M	T	U	E
V	A	E	C	R	A	T	E	R	X	N	E	V	L	S
Q	W	O	X	S	Z	S	Y	R	N	N	E	F	H	S
M	P	K	P	E	B	B	W	R	I	N	V	D	F	R
E	D	F	Z	V	J	M	G	B	U	W	W	G	I	B
Q	P	I	V	E	Q	P	A	S	O	C	E	K	U	L
R	E	A	D	N	L	C	G	A	R	S	R	J	I	I
J	X	I	L	G	N	D	X	C	O	C	Z	E	I	A
E	T	I	R	O	E	T	E	M	O	J	I	T	M	G
R	D	I	V	J	G	T	V	J	A	Q	R	U	Z	F

"If I didn't know better, I'd say I was looking at the moon. In some places, it's flat. In other places, there are huge craters," Luke observed.

"Mercury's craters may have been formed when meteorites, or small comets, crashed into the planet," D.I.D.G.E.T. shared. "The temperature on Mercury is 800 degrees Fahrenheit or 427 degrees Celcius."

"Why is it so hot?" Luke asked Addison.

"Mercury is three times closer to the sun than Earth is," Addison answered.

Suddenly, the pod began to rumble and shake as it had when it left the barn. Meteorites, rocks and other space dust were rocking it. Addison put the pod into high gear. Off to Venus!

Activity 2

Skill: Word Study

How many words can you make from the letters in the following word?

METEORITE

_____   _____

_____   _____

_____   _____

_____   _____

Plurals and Possessives

Plural words end in s. The s shows that there is more than one of something.

Possessive words end in 's. The 's shows that something belongs to someone or something.

In the sentences below, circle the words that are plural and add an apostrophe to the words that are possessive.

Example: The girls ran in the town's race.

1. The horses pulled the farmers wagon.

2. The kids sandbox had toys in it.

3. The girls kite was very far up in the air.

4. The cats kittens were fluffy and gray.

5. The boys went to their friends house.

6. The kids put the schools flag up every morning.

Factoid

Children in Japan are expected to take their studies very seriously. Children have a long school day and they attend class every day except for Sunday. In addition to their regular school requirements, many children also attend extra classes in the evening to prepare them for exams.

Safety Tip

Is there an adult at home? Whenever you answer the phone, be careful not to tell strangers that an adult is not at home. Tell them that an adult cannot come to the phone right now and that you may take a message. If someone knocks on the door when you are home alone, do not open the door.

Can you find...?

Circle the items hidden in the picture.

Beaker

Microscope

Flask

Addison

D.I.D.G.E.T.

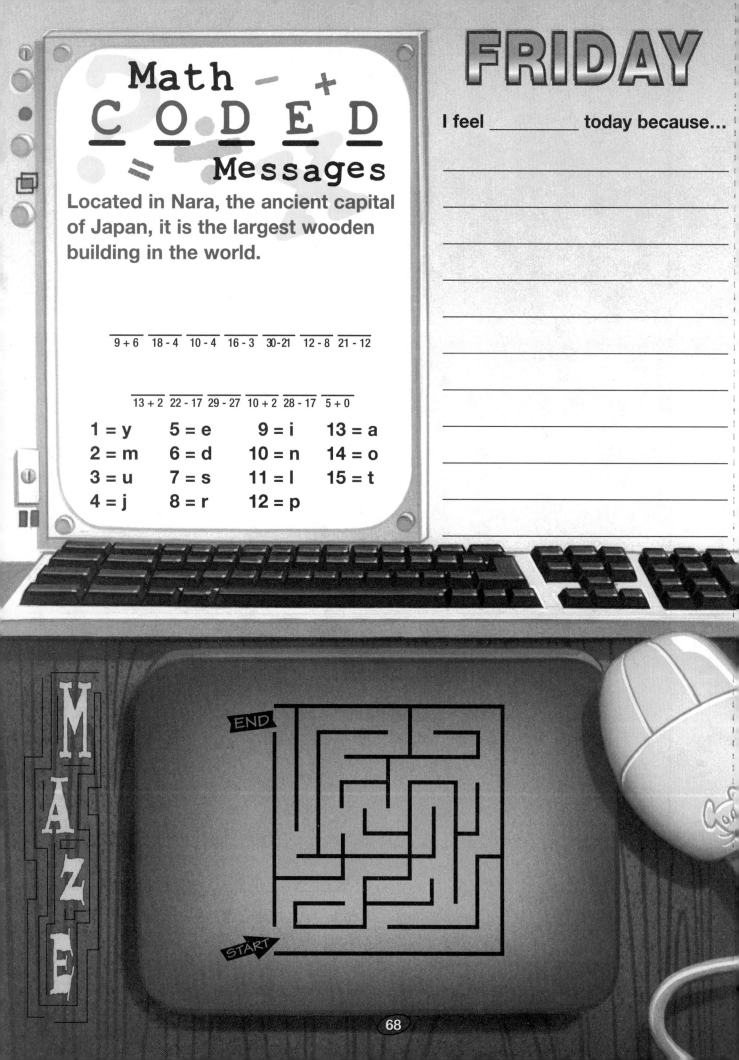

Math CODED Messages

Located in Nara, the ancient capital of Japan, it is the largest wooden building in the world.

$$\overline{}_{9+6}\ \overline{}_{18-4}\ \overline{}_{10-4}\ \overline{}_{16-3}\ \overline{}_{30-21}\ \overline{}_{12-8}\ \overline{}_{21-12}$$

$$\overline{}_{13+2}\ \overline{}_{22-17}\ \overline{}_{29-27}\ \overline{}_{10+2}\ \overline{}_{28-17}\ \overline{}_{5+0}$$

1 = y	5 = e	9 = i	13 = a
2 = m	6 = d	10 = n	14 = o
3 = u	7 = s	11 = l	15 = t
4 = j	8 = r	12 = p	

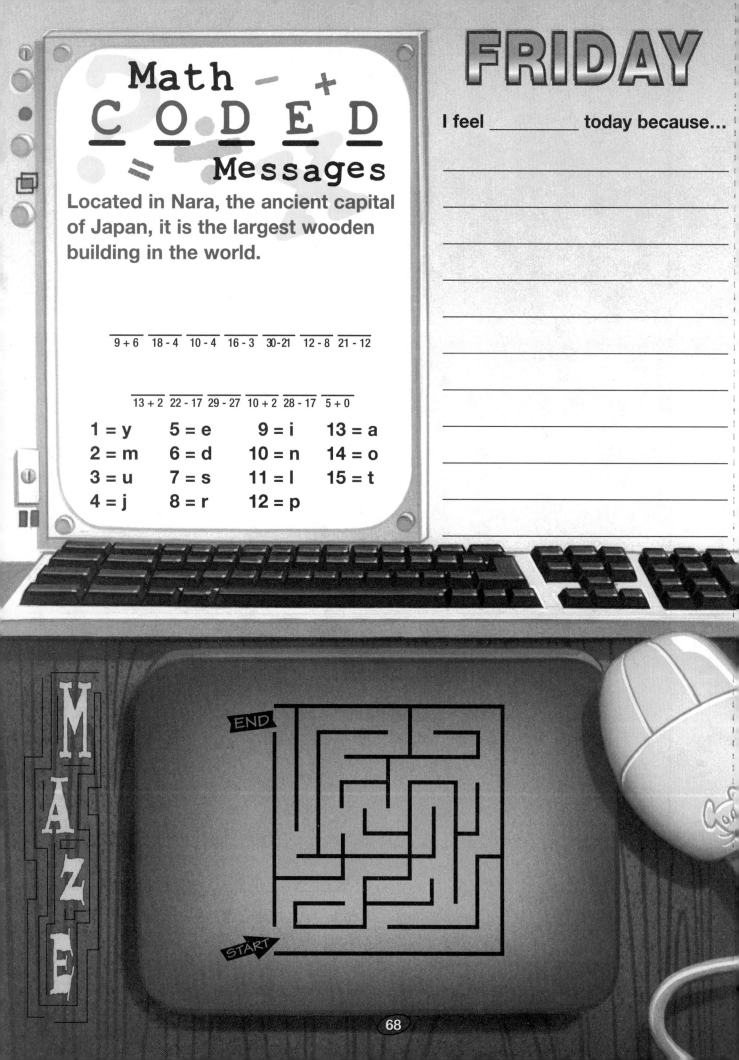
MAZE

END

START

FRIDAY

I feel _____ today because...

_____
_____
_____
_____
_____
_____
_____
_____
_____
_____
_____

Can you get the facts straight? Choose from these words to complete the story! Beware, there are extra words to make it more challenging!

label	rice	important	Godzilla
mountain	hopped	kite	largest
exclaimed	manufacture	robot	flag
baseball	smudge	temple	

Addison's mother looked at the pile of flags in the corner of the room. Then she looked at Addison. Addison knew what that meant.

"Come on, D.I.D.G.E.T.," Addison said. "We need to put more of these away. Let's get a box."

D.I.D.G.E.T. found a box with a picture on it. The picture was of a tall, snow-capped _____.

noun

"Play lots of _____ here," Addison read the first of the clues

noun
on the box. "_____ computers." Finally she read, "Build lots

verb
of cars."

"That sounds just like us," Addison said, reaching for the United States _____.

noun

"Beep-beep!" D.I.D.G.E.T. _____ up and down. "Beep-

verb
beep!" There was a fourth clue on a slip of paper inside the box. It read, "Island nation, fishing industry _____."

adjective

"We're not an island," puzzled Addison. "But who else can it be?" She looked closer at the box. A _____ under the picture of the

noun
mountain looked like more printing. She picked up her magnifying glass.

"Are we silly!" she _____. "We should have read the

verb
_____ first. The picture is of Mount Fuji, Japan's _____

noun   *adjective*
volcano. This box belongs to the Japanese flag!"

activity

Adult supervision is recommended.

Pipecleaner Clock

Materials:

paper plate

2 pipe cleaners

markers or crayons

pencil

Directions:

1 Using your pencil, lightly draw a straight line from the top of the paper plate to the bottom. Then lightly draw a straight line from the left of your plate to the right. This will divide your paper plate into four equal quarters. Use these lines to help you keep the numbers on the face of your clock spaced evenly. The point where the lines cross will be the middle of your clock.

2 Using markers or crayons, write a 12 at the top of your straight line. Then write a 6 at the bottom of your straight line. You can look at the clocks on the next page to help you.

3 Now write a 9 at the left of your other straight line and a 3 at the right of it.

4 Fill in the other numbers on your clock's face. Draw dashes for each number. Then fill in between the numbers with 4 smaller dashes.

5 Get an adult to help you poke a small hole in the center of your clock where the two pencil lines cross.

6 Cut your pipe cleaners so that you have one that is 3 1/2 inches long (9 cm) and one that is 2 inches long (6 cm).

7 Poke the pipe cleaners through the hole so that about a half inch (1 cm) sticks out the back and bend them down. These are the hands of your clock. Carefully bend down the tips of your clock's hands so they don't poke you. Then bend the hands down so they touch the face of the clock.

8 Use your new clock to practice telling time!

TELLING TIME

Record the correct time or draw hands on the clock to show the correct time.

4:04

_____

8:16

_____

2:55

_____

11:45

_____

Y as a Vowel

Sometimes Y acts as a vowel. Circle the correct spelling for the words below.

1. crie   cry   crye

2. baby   babby   babi

3. tri   trye   try

4. whi   why   whye

MATH

Can you fill in the yellow triangles with the correct signs to equal 9? Your choices are "+" and "–." The first one has been done for you.

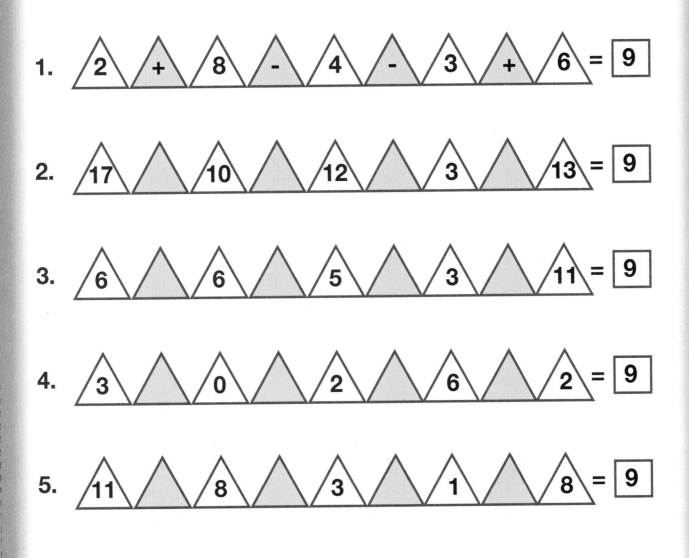

1. 2 + 8 – 4 – 3 + 6 = 9

2. 17   10   12   3   13 = 9

3. 6   6   5   3   11 = 9

4. 3   0   2   6   2 = 9

5. 11   8   3   1   8 = 9

Look at the map on page 60. Describe what you would expect to find in Japan…

_____

_____

_____

_____

_____

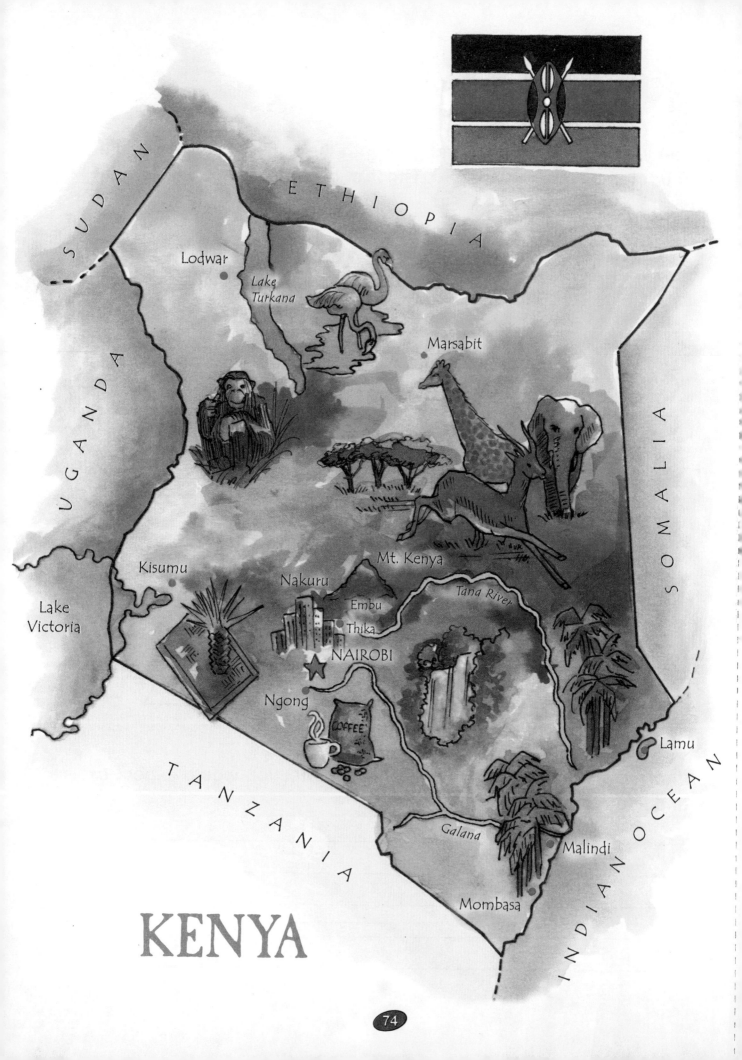

SUDAN

ETHIOPIA

UGANDA

Lodwar

Lake
Turkana

Marsabit

SOMALIA

Kisumu

Lake
Victoria

Nakuru

Mt. Kenya

Tana River

Embu

Thika

NAIROBI

Ngong

COFFEE

Galana

TANZANIA

Malindi

Mombasa

Lamu

INDIAN OCEAN

KENYA

FACTS ABOUT KENYA

Kenya is located in Eastern Africa next to the Indian Ocean. The central grassy plains of Kenya are called the savannahs. Lions and cheetahs both can be found in Kenya. Lions live in small groups called prides. The cheetah is the fastest-running animal on earth. Many people from all over the world enjoy going on safaris to see all the animals. The coffee bean is the main export crop of Kenya.

63

CROSSWORD

401

Across

1. The central grassy plains of Kenya are known as the _____. Many animals live and hunt here.

2. This bean, which is used for a popular drink, is the main export crop of Kenya.

3. Kenya is located next to the _____ Ocean on the eastern coast of Africa.

Down

1. These large animals found in Kenya live in small groups called prides.

2. Tourists come from all over the world to go on a _____, or journey, to see the wildlife in Kenya's famous game parks.

3. These are the fastest-running animals on earth.

Make a Model of the Solar System: Mars

Adult supervision is recommended.

Materials

$1\frac{1}{2}$" (3.8 cm) foam ball
6" (15.2 cm) piece of
    medium-gauge wire
ruler
red acrylic (water-based) paint
paintbrush
craft glue
scissors
old newspapers
model from the previous activity
play putty or modeling clay
toothpick

Mars, also known as the Red Planet, is the fourth planet from the sun. The dirt on Mars contains clay that is rich in iron. The iron gives Mars its characteristic red color. Mars is a rocky planet that has many volcanoes, including Olympus Mons, the largest volcano in our solar system! Mars also has very cold temperatures, usually around -85 degrees Fahrenheit (-65 degrees Celsius) even on the warmest days. The Red Planet is about half the size of Earth.

Directions

1. Spread clean newspapers on a table.

2. Push a toothpick into the foam ball.

3. Hold the foam ball by the toothpick, and paint the entire ball with red paint.

4. Gently push the toothpick into putty or modeling clay so the ball will dry without touching anything. Place the painted ball on a clean spot on the newspaper.

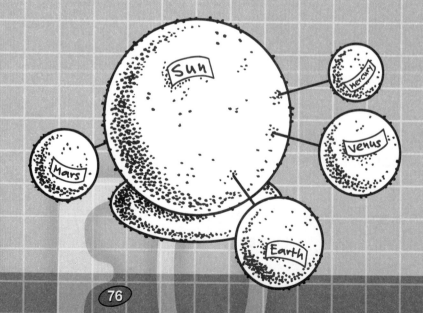

Mars

5. Let the ball dry for about five hours.

6. Cut out the Mars label on the previous page, and glue it to the dried Mars planet model.

7. Measure the wire so that it is 6" (15.2 cm) long. Have an adult break or cut the wire to the correct length.

8. Put glue on one end of the wire. Push the wire about $\frac{1}{2}$" (1.3 cm) into the Mars planet.

9. Put glue on the other end of the wire. Push 1" (2.5 cm) of the wire attached to Mars into the Sun model about $1\frac{1}{8}$" (2.9 cm) from the Earth wire.

Extension

The only known life in our solar system is on Earth. However, many scientists believe that Mars may have been like Earth in the past, when it contained water. Today, Mars has large frozen ice caps, but no liquid water. Imagine there being life on another planet! On the lines below, write a story about what life forms on Mars may have been like.

_____

_____

_____

_____

_____

_____

_____

_____

_____

All Aboard the Space Pod

Chapter 6

"We are now coming up to Earth's twin," D.I.D.G.E.T. announced.

Luke looked through his Super Scope. "All I can see are clouds."

Addison used the control pad close to the window to steer the pod out of the clouds.

"Venus is called Earth's twin because it is closest to Earth in size," Addison explained.

"Thanks, Add. Hey, look over there! Venus has mountains and even volcanoes," Luke exclaimed.

Addison turned toward D.I.D.G.E.T. and read the data on his computer screen. "More than half the planet's surface is flat. In other places there are mountains and craters. Some mountains are seven miles high."

Luke could only whistle in amazement.

Activity 1

Skill: Reading Comprehension

Answer the following questions on the lines provided.

1. Why does Addison need to move the Space Pod?

_____

2. Why is Venus called Earth's twin?

_____

3. How tall are some of the mountains on Venus?

_____

4. Describe the surface of Venus.

_____

"Can we land and climb some of the mountains?" Luke asked.

Addison shook her head. "Remember when we went to the plant store with Dad?" she asked. "And remember how hot it was in the greenhouse?"

Luke nodded. "Yeah, we were all sweaty when we came out."

"The surface of Venus is like a greenhouse. The clouds trap the sun's warmth near the surface. This makes Venus hotter than Mercury," Addison explained.

Luke looked sadly at the swirling clouds. Addison patted his hand. She let him press the buttons on the control pad to steer the pod to their next planet.

Activity 2

Skill: Similes

Similes use the words *like* or *as* to compare things that are alike. They are used to explain or give more description in writing. Example: "He was as quiet as a mouse."

1. What two things are compared in this chapter?

_____

2. What other similes can you think of?

_____

_____

_____

HOMONYMS

Homonyms are words that sound alike but are spelled different and mean different things. Listed below are a group of statements about the picture on page 81. Circle the correct homonym for each statement.

1. The son/sun is shining.

2. There are for/four flowers near the rhinoceros.

3. In Kenya, the whether/weather is hot.

4. Most of the people have bare/bear feet.

5. Two palm trees have grown/groan near the beach.

6. The jogger is wearing a pair/pear of white shoes.

Factoid

Storytellers in Kenya are highly respected. Children learn traditions, history and lessons by listening to people tell the many different folktales, legends and myths of the Kenyan culture—or just stories of a person's past. Many Kenyans in rural areas don't have TV—or even electricity—so children often gather in the evening in the home of a good storyteller to hear tales.

Safety Tip

Do you know important phone numbers? Create an emergency phone number list with help from an adult. Write down the phone numbers of the fire department, the police department, and relatives. Place this list by the telephone so you will have it in case of an emergency.

Can you find...?

Circle the items hidden in the picture.

Beaker

Microscope

Flask

Addison

D.I.D.G.E.T.

Math CODED Messages

The two main languages spoken in Kenya are:

$$\overline{8+4}\ \overline{30-20}\ \overline{9+7}\ \overline{12+3}\ \overline{19-11}\ \overline{18-5}\ \overline{6+2}$$

and

$$\overline{28-14}\ \overline{9+2}\ \overline{20-17}\ \overline{8+5}\ \overline{17-9}\ \overline{6+6}\ \overline{45-30}$$

1 = d	6 = p	11 = n	16 = a
2 = b	7 = c	12 = s	17 = q
3 = g	8 = i	13 = l	
4 = m	9 = a	14 = e	
5 = o	10 = w	15 = h	

I feel _____ today because...

_____

_____

_____

_____

_____

_____

_____

_____

_____

MAZE

END

START

Can you get the facts straight? Choose from these words to complete the story! Beware, there are extra words to make it more challenging!

travel	complained	found	gorilla
treasures	trip	zoo	listen
animals	village	language	wondered
fierce	picture	sitting	

On Safari

"It's raining," _____ Addison.
verb

"Good," replied Addison's mother. "This is an attic day. We'll go into the attic and _____ to the rain while we hunt for _____."
verb   noun

Soon Addison was _____ in the middle of the attic floor. "Look
verb

what I _____," she said, waving a wide-brimmed hat. "This is like
verb

what explorers wear. It goes with these." She pointed to books full of

pictures of strange _____."
noun

"You're right," her mother said. "That's a safari hat. Those books were

written long ago by a woman who went on a safari in Kenya. 'Safari'

means journey in Swahili—the _____ many people in Kenya
noun

speak."

"A long time ago—I guess that's why all her pictures are black and

white. Do these animals still live in Kenya?" _____ Addison. There
verb

were pictures of lions and leopards and cheetahs—and elephants and

hippos and rhinos. There were zebras and giraffes and hyenas—and

gazelles and buffaloes and wildebeests. There even was a _____
noun

of an ostrich.

"They certainly do. Maybe someday you can go there and see them."

"I'm not going to wait," said Addison. "It won't be like really going to

Kenya, but I'm going to wear my safari hat the next time we go to the

_____!"
noun

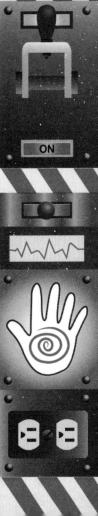

83

activity

Adult supervision is recommended.

Layered Bean Jar

Directions:

① Spoon a 1-inch (3 cm) layer of beans into the jar.

② Use a different kind of bean and carefully add a second layer. Pat it down and add other layers in the same way until the jar is very full and tight.

③ Put on the lid.

④ Glue ribbon around the lid.

⑤ Make a bow. Put a dot of glue on the back of the bow and glue it to the ribbon.

Materials:

glass jar with screw-
  on lid

dried beans
  (3 to 4 kinds)

ribbon

spoon

non-toxic white glue

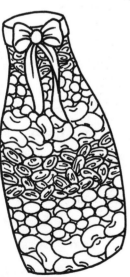

MATH PUZZLE

Solve the equations below to complete the puzzle. Remember to do the work in each set of parentheses ( ) first. Write the letter that matches the correct answer on the lines below.

D (11+3) – (6+6)

I (25+5) + (16-14)

N (18-6) + (42-32)

A (89-79) + (13+5)

S (44+4) – (12+12)

G (7-7) + (36-5)

O (8+10) – (4+5)

E (15+5) + (20+20)

T (13+3) – (4+4)

<u>28</u> <u>2</u> <u>2</u> <u>32</u> <u>24</u> <u>9</u> <u>22</u>   <u>28</u> <u>22</u> <u>2</u>

<u>2</u> <u>32</u> <u>2</u> <u>31</u> <u>60</u> <u>8</u>

Soft C vs. Hard C

The letter c can have two sounds. Soft c = s sound. Hard c = k sound. Circle hard or soft next to each word to show if it uses a soft c or a hard c.

1. cat   hard/soft

2. candy   hard/soft

3. celery   hard/soft

4. city   hard/soft

5. crib   hard/soft

6. cider   hard/soft

MATH

Can you fill in the blanks with the correct sign to equal 14?
Your choices are "+" and "–." The first one has been done for you.

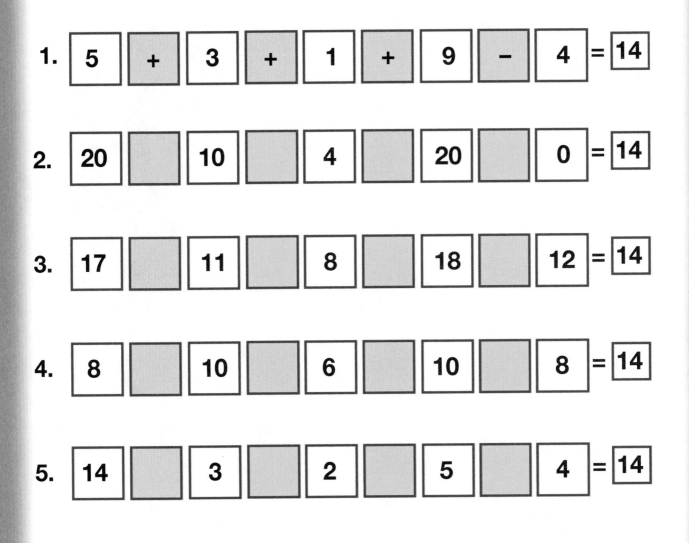

1. 5 + 3 + 1 + 9 – 4 = 14

2. 20 [ ] 10 [ ] 4 [ ] 20 [ ] 0 = 14

3. 17 [ ] 11 [ ] 8 [ ] 18 [ ] 12 = 14

4. 8 [ ] 10 [ ] 6 [ ] 10 [ ] 8 = 14

5. 14 [ ] 3 [ ] 2 [ ] 5 [ ] 4 = 14

Look at the map on page 74. Describe what you would expect to find in Kenya…

_____

_____

_____

_____

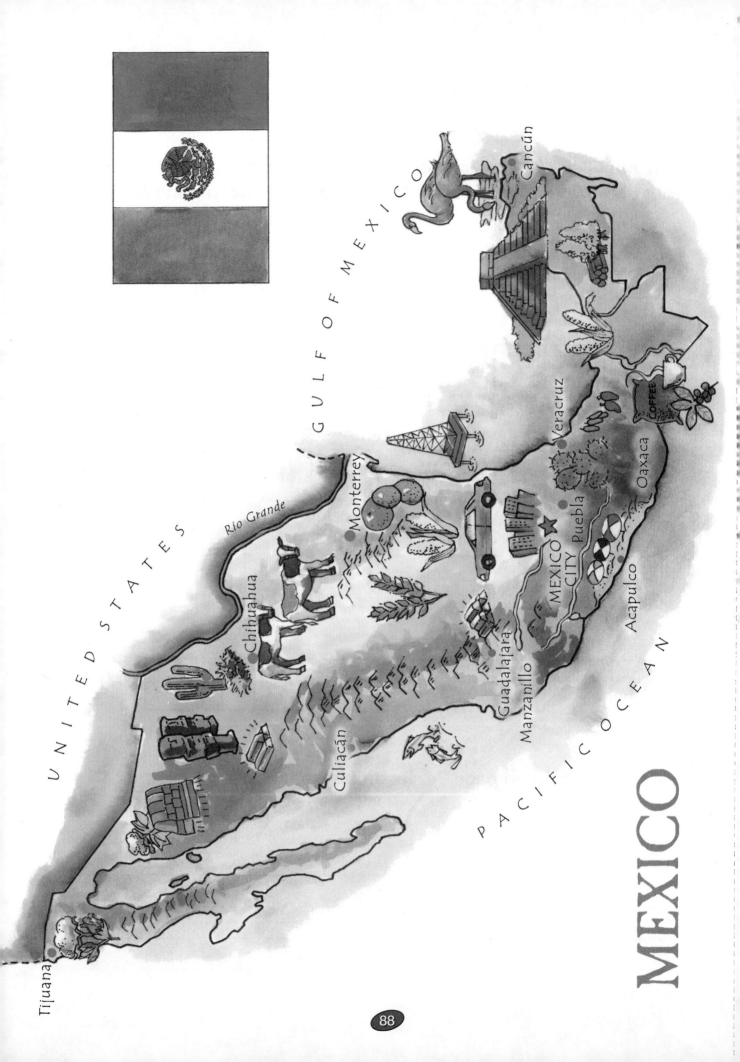

Cancún

GULF OF MEXICO

Veracruz

Oaxaca

COFFEE

Monterrey

Puebla

MEXICO CITY

Rio Grande

Acapulco

Chihuahua

UNITED STATES

Guadalajara

Manzanillo

PACIFIC OCEAN

Culiacán

MEXICO

Tijuana

88

FACTS ABOUT MEXICO

Mexico is located in the southern portion of North America. The Pacific Ocean and the Gulf of Mexico border it. The ancient Mayan civilization of Mexico developed a very accurate calendar. Some of the plants and animals native to Mexico include cactus, iguanas and flamingos. Beans are a staple part of the Mexican diet.

63

CROSSWORD

Across

1. Mexico is bordered by the Pacific Ocean and the _____ of Mexico.
2. The ancient Mayan civilization of Mexico devised a very accurate _____ to measure the passage of days and years.

Down

1. A spiky plant found in Mexico. It stores water in its stem and can survive in climates where very little rain falls.

2. A staple of the Mexican diet, these are eaten boiled, in soups, on tortillas, fried or refried.

3. These large green lizards have a row of scales running down their backs. They can be found in the Mexican tropics and are sometimes kept as pets.

4. These long-legged pink birds feed in the swamps of Mexico's Yucatan Peninsula.

Make a Model of the Solar System: Jupiter

Adult supervision is recommended.

Materials

4" (10.2 cm) foam ball
7" (17.8 cm) piece of
   medium-gauge wire
ruler
red acrylic (water-based) paint
white acrylic (water-based) paint
paintbrush
craft glue
scissors
old newspapers
model from the previous activity
play putty or modeling clay
toothpick

Jupiter is the largest planet in our solar system—11 times bigger than Earth! If you could travel to Jupiter, you would not be able to stand on the planet because it is not solid: Jupiter is made of icy, cold gases that are usually around -243.67 degrees Fahrenheit (-153.15 degrees Celsius). Jupiter has 16 moons and a colorful ring system that is made of dust.

Directions

1. Cover a table with newspapers.

2. Push a toothpick into the foam ball.

3. Hold the foam ball by the toothpick, and paint the entire ball with pink paint. You can make pink by mixing a tiny bit of red paint with white paint.

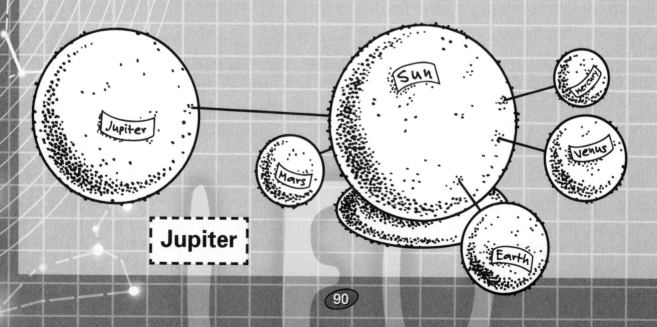

Jupiter

4. Gently push the toothpick into putty or modeling clay so the ball will dry without touching anything. Place the painted ball on a clean spot on the newspaper.

5. Let the ball dry for about five hours.

6. Cut out the Jupiter label on the previous page, and glue it to the dried Jupiter planet model.

7. Measure the wire so that it is 7" (17.8 cm) long. Have an adult break or cut the wire to the correct length.

8. Put glue on one end of the wire. Push the wire about $\frac{1}{2}$" (1.3 cm) into the Jupiter planet.

9. Put glue on the other end of the wire. Push 1" (2.5 cm) of the wire attached to Jupiter into the sun model about $2\frac{1}{8}$" (5.4 cm) from the Mars wire.

Extension

Find pictures of Jupiter in a book or magazine. You'll see that it is really a colorful planet! Jupiter looks striped because of the different molecules in its air. Use different colors of paint to make these stripes on your model of Jupiter. Or, use markers or colored pencils to draw Jupiter in the space below.

All Aboard the Space Pod

Chapter 7

"The next planet within our view is Earth," D.I.D.G.E.T. announced.

"We could land and explore this planet," Addison teased.

"Let's save the exploring for when we go home," Luke begged. "Let's go to Mars. I just know we can land on Mars."

"Well, if we are going to land, we'll need to gear up," Addison replied.

Addison floated over to a closet. She pulled out two silver space suits. She handed one suit to Luke and put the other suit on.

"How do I look?" Luke said as he kicked his puffy legs.

Addison returned to her seat, trying hard not to laugh.

Activity 1

Skill: Word Search

Verbs show action. Find the verbs from the word bank that are hidden in the puzzle. Words can be vertical, horizontal or diagonal.

ANNOUNCED

FALL

HURRY

RUMBLE

DETERMINED

GUIDE

KICKED

SHAKE

EXPLORED

HIKED

LAND

D	O	C	B	W	T	Z	T	G	R	I	J	L	C	J
S	E	F	M	C	D	Q	Q	S	E	Z	J	L	N	H
L	C	N	L	E	V	Z	Y	Q	U	X	S	W	S	S
X	N	W	I	M	L	T	A	L	A	D	B	J	F	Z
M	U	K	U	M	N	E	L	G	S	W	I	X	K	J
K	O	E	G	X	R	A	S	U	N	W	X	C	R	T
K	N	T	T	R	F	E	M	I	E	N	H	A	L	H
W	N	E	S	Q	K	N	T	D	H	K	T	W	I	G
R	A	X	G	S	W	I	E	E	D	Y	W	W	I	Q
X	X	F	H	G	H	R	C	C	D	E	V	J	O	U
M	C	A	I	V	O	M	B	K	W	J	K	V	M	D
L	K	F	N	L	Q	J	M	B	E	M	W	I	C	N
E	A	M	P	R	U	M	B	L	E	D	P	A	H	A
C	U	X	Y	R	R	U	H	C	L	J	S	R	H	L
O	E	E	K	A	Y	U	P	O	K	X	G	R	L	A

Addison guided the pod past Earth and in the direction of Mars. Because this was their first landing, Addison crossed her fingers and hoped it would be smooth.

"Buckle up, Luke," Addison directed.

The pod landed with only a little rattling. The door opened, and Luke hurried out. He was determined to find water—real Martian water.

"I'll see you, Add. I'm sure I saw a river over there," Luke said as he hiked off. He kicked his toe into the reddish-orange dirt every few steps.

"Don't fall into any craters," called Addison.

Activity 2

Skill: Compare and Contrast

Addison and Luke have visited three planets so far. Record their observations here.

Mercury	Venus	Mars

Correct The Sentences

Listed below are a group of sentences that relate to the picture on page 95. Correct the punctuation and use capital letters where needed for each sentence. (Remember, the first word of a sentence and proper nouns begin with capital letters.)

1. mexico is surrounded by the pacific ocean and the gulf of mexico

2. have you ever seen a bullfighter

3. chili peppers are used in mexican dishes

4. there are many beautiful beaches in mexico

Factoid

The ancient Aztec Indians of Mexico were well-known warriors. They believed that if they made human sacrifices to their gods, they would be blessed with good crops, good weather and victory in war.

Safety Tip

Do you wear your seat belt? Riding safely in a car is very important. Never hang your arms or legs out of the window. Always wear your seat belt. Also, make sure that all babies are seated in a car seat, and that all adults are wearing their seat belts, too!

Can you find...?

Circle the items hidden in the picture.

Beaker

Microscope

Flask

Addison

D.I.D.G.E.T.

Math CODED Messages

I am home to the Copper Canyon—
so deep that four Grand Canyons
could fit inside.

___ ___ ___ ___ ___ ___ ___ ___ ___
22 - 7 32 - 20 5 + 6 28 - 16 7 + 0 11 - 2 9 + 3 22 - 15 27 - 18

1 = m	5 = l	9 = a	13 = g
2 = s	6 = y	10 = o	14 = p
3 = n	7 = u	11 = i	15 = c
4 = t	8 = e	12 = h	

I feel _____ today because…

_____
_____
_____
_____
_____
_____
_____
_____
_____
_____
_____

MAZE

START

END

Can you get the facts straight? Choose from these words to complete the story! Beware, there are extra words to make it more challenging!

piñata	large	built	head
shaped	grabbed	tortilla	feathers
lifted	papier-mâche	rain	attic
breaks	tail	toys	

Party Time!

Addison looked outdoors. It wasn't raining, but it was cool enough to go back into the _____. She wanted to open a big trunk she'd
        noun
found.

It was a very big trunk. Inside it, she saw a _____, heavy-looking
                            adjective
orange ball. Addison braced her feet, _____ hard, and nearly fell
                              verb
over backwards. The ball was so big that her arms would not reach
around it, but it was made of _____ and was very light. It rattled.
                        noun

One end of the ball was _____ to look like a chicken's head.
                     verb
At the other side there was a place to stick feathers, like a _____.
                                              noun
In between, Addison found a place to put a string. She looked inside
the trunk again. There were the _____. She _____ them and
                         noun   *adjective*
ran downstairs.

"Look! I found a piñata!" Addison called.

Her friend Tommy was playing with D.I.D.G.E.T. "What's a piñata?"
Tommy asked.

"It's from Mexico. It's for parties. It's full of candy and prizes. We
hang it way up high with this string. Then we wear blindfolds and hit the
_____ with sticks until someone _____ it. All the prizes fall out,
  noun   *verb*
and we get to keep them!"

"Great!" said Tommy. "My birthday's tomorrow. Bring it to my party!"

# activity

Adult supervision is recommended.

Note Holder

Directions:

1 Glue a clothespin to the back of a small tile.

2 Let it dry completely.

3 Stand the tile on the clothespin.

4 Clip notes to the tile.

Materials:

3" x 3"
  (8 cm x 8 cm)
  ceramic tile

clothespin

craft glue

COUNTING MONEY

$1.00 (one dollar) = 100 pennies

$1.00 (one dollar) =   20 nickels

$1.00 (one dollar) =   10 dimes

$1.00 (one dollar) =   4 quarters

Each grouping of coins needs to add to one dollar. Fill in the missing amounts for each.

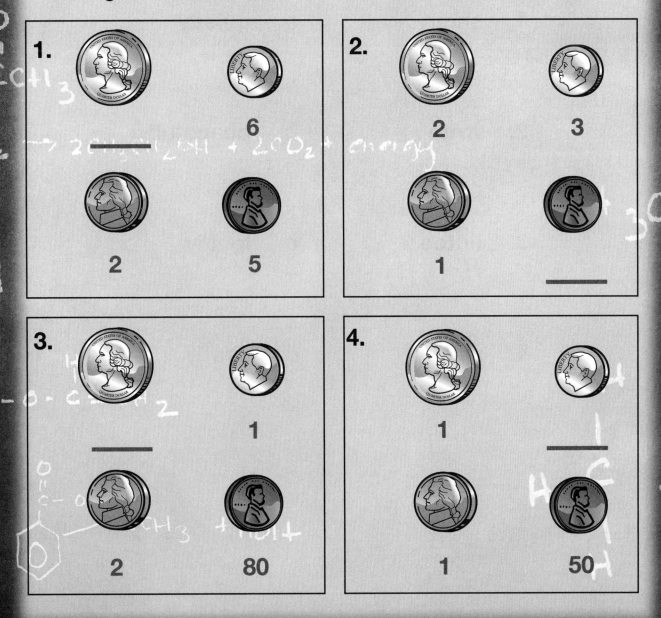

1.

6

2   5

2.

2   3

1   ___

3.

2

___

2   80

4.

1   1

1   50

Adverbs

Adverbs are words that describe verbs. They often end in **ly**. Match the correct verbs and adverbs below by drawing lines between them.

1. shout   a. quietly

2. write   b. peacefully

3. tiptoe   c. loudly

4. sleep   d. neatly

MATH

Can you fill in the blanks with the correct sign to equal 8?
Your choices are "+" and "−." The first one has been done for you.

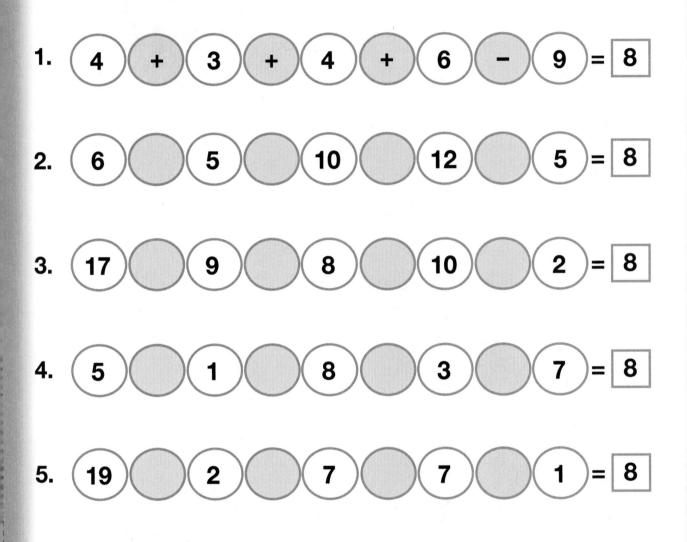

1. (4)(+)(3)(+)(4)(+)(6)(−)(9) = [8]

2. (6)(   )(5)(   )(10)(   )(12)(   )(5) = [8]

3. (17)(   )(9)(   )(8)(   )(10)(   )(2) = [8]

4. (5)(   )(1)(   )(8)(   )(3)(   )(7) = [8]

5. (19)(   )(2)(   )(7)(   )(7)(   )(1) = [8]

Look at the map on page 88. Describe what you would expect to find in Mexico...

_____

_____

_____

_____

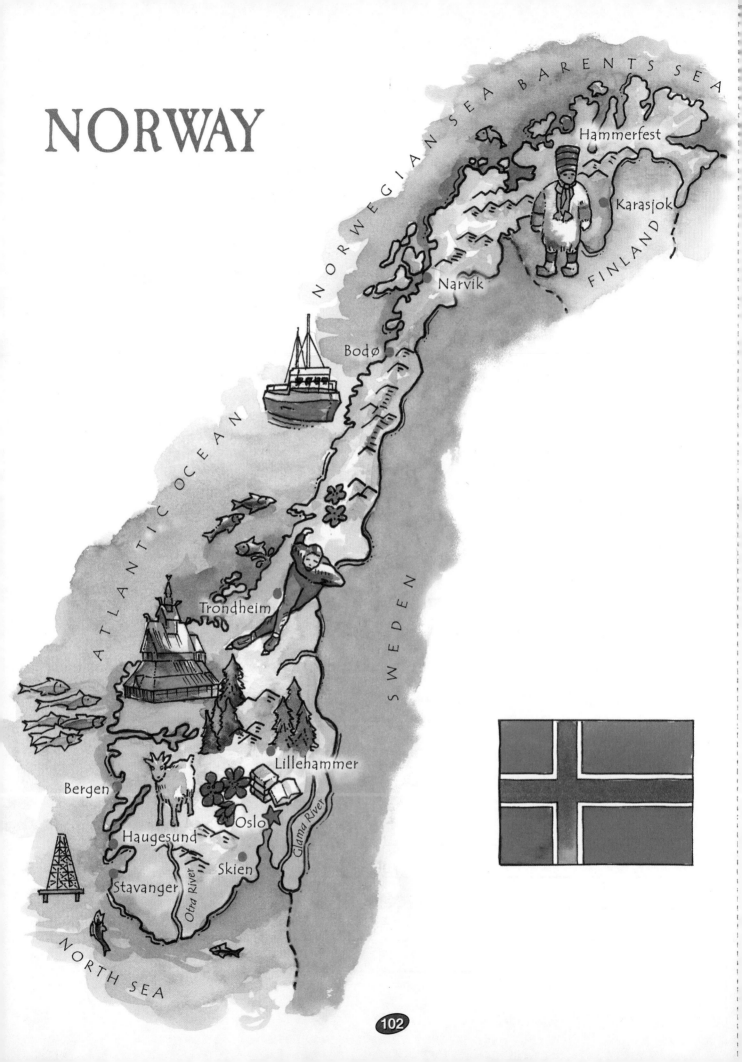

NORWAY

NORWEGIAN SEA

BARENTS SEA

Hammerfest

Karasjok

FINLAND

Narvik

Bodø

ATLANTIC OCEAN

Trondheim

SWEDEN

Bergen

Lillehammer

Glama River

Oslo

Haugesund

Skien

Ofra River

Stavanger

NORTH SEA

FACTS ABOUT

NORWAY

Norway is located in Northern Europe. The Atlantic Ocean, Sweden and Finland border it. Norway was once covered with glaciers. Fjords, which are narrow waterways between steep, rocky cliffs, can be found there. Reindeer are native animals to Norway. Norway is unique because the sun doesn't set during the summer. The Vikings of Norway discovered America before Christopher Columbus.

63

CROSSWORD

Across

1. A fjord is a narrow waterway between steep, rocky _____. They're caused by glacial erosion.

2. Norway is known as "the land of the midnight sun" because the sun doesn't set during this season.

3. A large animal found in Norway that has hooves and antlers.

4. Norway was once covered with _____, which are enormous masses of ice. They helped to form the thousands of lakes that exist throughout the country today.

Down

1. These early explorers were fierce warriors who discovered America before Christopher Columbus.

2. A country that borders Norway.

Make a Model of the Solar System: Saturn

Adult supervision is recommended.

Materials

- 3" (7.6 cm) foam ball
- 4 $\frac{1}{2}$" (11.4 cm) foam ring
- 8" (20.3 cm) piece of medium-gauge wire
- ruler
- yellow acrylic (water-based) paint
- red acrylic (water-based) paint
- white acrylic (water-based) paint
- paintbrush
- craft glue
- scissors
- old newspapers
- model from the previous activity
- play putty or modeling clay
- toothpicks

Directions

1. Spread clean newspapers over a table.
2. Push a toothpick into the foam ball and a toothpick into the foam ring.
3. Hold the foam ball by the toothpick, and paint the entire ball with yellow paint.

If you look closely, you can see the bright rings around Saturn on a clear night. The rings are made of ice and dust. Some scientists think the particles in the rings formed when moons circling Saturn were destroyed. Saturn is more than nine times larger than Earth. Its center is hot and its rings are icy-cold, with an average temperature of -301.27degrees Fahrenheit (-185.15 degrees Celsius). Saturn is a very windy planet. The winds there sometimes reach 1,000 mi. (1,609.3 km) per hour!

Saturn

4. Gently push the toothpick into putty or modeling clay so the ball will dry without touching anything. Place the painted ball on a clean spot on the newspaper.

5. Hold the foam ring by the toothpick, and paint the entire ring with pink paint. You can use a mixture of white paint with a tiny bit of red.

6. Push the toothpick into putty or modeling clay, and place the painted ring on a clean spot on the newspaper. Let the foam ball and ring dry for about five hours.

7. Gently push the dried pink ring onto the dried Saturn model until it is around the center of Saturn.

8. Cut out the Saturn label on the previous page, and glue it to the dried Saturn planet model.

9. Measure the wire so that it is 8" (20.3 cm) long. Have an adult break or cut the wire to the correct length.

10. Put glue on one end of the wire. Push the wire about $\frac{1}{2}$" (1.3 cm) under the ring and into the Saturn planet.

11. Put glue on the other end of the wire. Push 1" (2.5 cm) of the wire attached to Saturn into the sun model about $3\frac{1}{2}$" (8.9 cm) from the Jupiter wire.

Extension

In addition to its system of rings, Saturn has 28 moons! The planet's most significant moons are listed in the chart below. At your local library, find at least two facts about each of these moons. Write the facts in the chart.

Moon	Facts
Titan	
Mimas	
Iapetus	
Hyperion	

All Aboard the Space Pod

Chapter 8

On Mars, Addison collected soil samples near the Space Pod. She wanted to compare the soil on Mars with the soil on Earth.

"The temperature is 28 degrees Fahrenheit, or -2 degrees Celcius. I am showing frozen water about three feet below the surface," D.I.D.G.E.T. reported.

Luke made his way back to Addison and D.I.D.G.E.T., kicking rocks along the way. "All I want is some water bubbling up out of the ground," Luke complained as he kicked another rock. Suddenly, something sparkly caught his attention. Could it be?

Activity 1

Skill: Story Elements

Answer the following questions on the lines provided.

1. What is the *title*, or name, of this story?

   _____

2. The *setting* is where a story takes place. What is the setting for most of this story?

   _____

3. Who are the *characters*, or people, in this story?

   _____

4. Name one challenge or problem in this story. How do you think this challenge or problem will be resolved?

   _____

5. How do you think this story will end?

   _____

"Yes! Addison! I found it! It's ice! I found it!" Luke yelled. He pulled a bag out of his suit and scratched some of the frozen dirt into the bag.

"Addison, look! It's ice. It was right here," Luke said.

"This is fantastic, Luke. Did you get a good sample?" Addison asked.

"I think so. Hey, what's that?" Luke had seen a flash of light. Visions of aliens flashed through his head.

"Oh, no!" cried Addison. "Look at the Space Pod. It's getting ready for takeoff. Everybody run!"

Activity 2

Skill: Sequence of Events
Number these events in the order in which they happened.

_____ **1.** Addison collects soil samples.

_____ **2.** Luke finds ice.

_____ **3.** Luke looks for water.

_____ **4.** The children run for the Space Pod.

_____ **5.** Luke sees a flash of light.

Past Tense Verbs

When you add a **d**, or **ed**, to most verbs, you are writing about something that already happened. Listed below are sentences about the picture on page 109. Rewrite the sentences as past tense by adding **d** or **ed** to the verbs. Note: If the verb ends with **s**, you need to drop the **s** before adding **d** or **ed**. The first one has been done for you.

1. The bear floats down the river.

<u>The bear floated down the river.</u>

2. The Vikings wave at everyone.

_____

3. The fish jumps out of the water.

_____

4. The man skis down the mountain.

_____

5. The boats sail in the river.

_____

Factoid

Norway is famous for skiing. Almost everyone in Norway knows how to ski. Children are taught how to ski almost as soon as they can walk.

Safety Tip

Appliances can be dangerous! Be careful when you are using appliances around the house. It is very easy to get burned by a toaster, oven or barbecue grill. Always keep your distance and do not place towels or other cloth materials near the heat or flame. If you are using one of these appliances, ask an adult for help.

Can you find...?

Circle the items hidden in the picture.

Beaker

Microscope

Flask

Addison

D.I.D.G.E.T.

Math C̲O̲D̲E̲D̲ Messages

Almost one-half of Norway lies within this:

$$\overline{} \quad \overline{} \quad \overline{} \quad \overline{} \quad \overline{} \quad \overline{}$$
18 - 14   2 + 4   15 - 6   18 - 3   32 - 21   7 + 2

$$\overline{} \quad \overline{} \quad \overline{} \quad \overline{} \quad \overline{} \quad \overline{}$$
27 - 18   8 + 3   26- 20   5 + 4   24 - 11   30 - 18

1 = d	5 = j	9 = c	13 = l
2 = g	6 = r	10 = n	14 = m
3 = f	7 = s	11 = i	15 = t
4 = a	8 = q	12 = e	

I feel _____ today because...

_____

_____

_____

_____

_____

_____

_____

_____

_____

_____

MAZE

START

END

Can you get the facts straight? Choose from these words to complete the story! Beware, there are extra words to make it more challenging!

dragons	reindeer	yelled	noises
long	fish	threw	game
jagged	horns	Vikings	tape
spoon	map		

Spoons and Dragon-Ships

"Mom's going to be mad if we don't finish the flags," said Addison. "Shall we play the box _____ again?" She grabbed a silver-colored
<u>noun</u>
box and looked at its cover.

"Oh, get real!" she said. "This box says the ships here used to look like

_____!" She _____ the box back onto the pile.
<u>noun</u>   <u>verb</u>
D.I.D.G.E.T. made a lot of noises.

"Oh, all right," sighed Addison. She picked up the box again. "I'll see what else it says."

"The _____ came from here."
   <u>noun</u>
"Fjords. So what's a fjord?"

D.I.D.G.E.T. made more beeping _____ and spit out a _____
     <u>noun</u>   <u>adjective</u>
piece of tape. Addison tore the _____ off and read it.
       <u>noun</u>

"Oh!" she cried. "Vikings came from Norway, and Viking ships sometimes had dragons' heads carved onto their fronts. A fjord is a long arm of the sea reaching up into the land. That means they'd have lots of places to put dragon-ships, wouldn't they?"

"It says something more, though. The box says that the country is

shaped like a _____. Do you have a _____, D.I.D.G.E.T.?"
     <u>noun</u>   <u>noun</u>
D.I.D.G.E.T. lit up his display. There was Norway, looking just like a

spoon with _____ edges.
    <u>adjective</u>
"OH-KAY!" said Addison happily. And she put the Norway flag in its box.

activity

Adult supervision is recommended.

Hand-Painted Pencil Holder

Materials:

glass ivy bowl or
  round glass jar

acrylic paint:
  white, green,
  purple, and blue

paintbrush

Directions:

1 Paint stems and leaves around the outside of the bowl. Let it dry.

2 Paint alternating blue, white and purple flowers on the stems. Let the flowers dry.

3 Finish the design by adding white, purple and blue dots all around the flowers.

4 When the project is dry, give it to someone as a gift.

HELP ADDISON FIND D.I.D.G.E.T.

Start Here
Count by fives.

20	0	30	40	50	65	90	100	35	10
5	5	10	15	30	45	60	75	80	85
70	25	50	20	15	30	25	45	25	30
65	50	30	25	45	70	45	50	20	35
60	55	35	65	55	60	65	55	15	5
70	50	40	45	50	40	70	60	10	100
80	35	30	60	65	70	75	80	80	95
75	40	45	70	55	65	75	85	90	70
85	50	35	80	60	50	70	80	95	80
95	65	25	10	20	55	65	90	100	50

End Here

Parts of Speech

Match each part of speech to the correct word.

1. noun   a. pretty

2. article   b. Sally

3. verb   c. we

4. adjective   d. quickly

5. adverb   e. an

6. pronoun   f. walk

MATH

Can you fill in the blanks with the correct sign to equal 0?
Your choices are "+" and "-." The first one has been done for you.

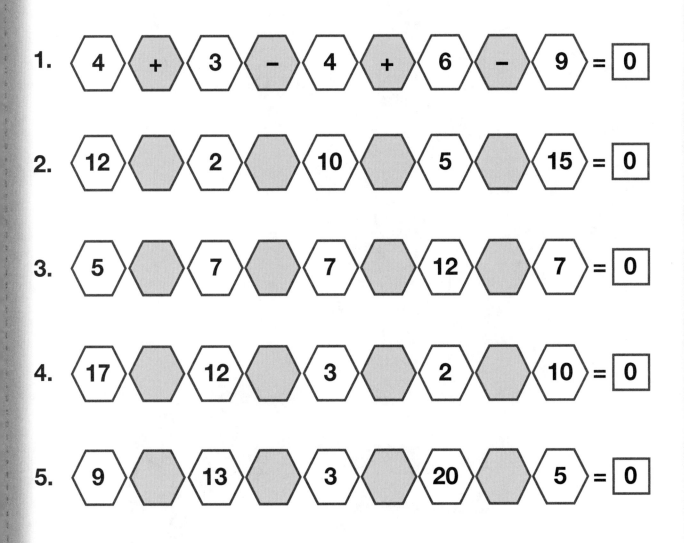

1. 4 + 3 – 4 + 6 – 9 = 0

2. 12 ◇ 2 ◇ 10 ◇ 5 ◇ 15 = 0

3. 5 ◇ 7 ◇ 7 ◇ 12 ◇ 7 = 0

4. 17 ◇ 12 ◇ 3 ◇ 2 ◇ 10 = 0

5. 9 ◇ 13 ◇ 3 ◇ 20 ◇ 5 = 0

Look at the map on page 102. Describe what you would expect to find in Norway…

_____

_____

_____

_____

_____

PERU

Tumbes

ECUADOR

COLOMBIA

Iquitos

Amazon River

COFFEE

Chiclayo

Andes

BRAZIL

Trujillo

Chimbote

Ucayali River

PACIFIC OCEAN

Callao
LIMA

Huancayo

Machu Picchu

Pisco

Cuzco

Andes

BOLIVIA

Arequipa

Puno

Lake Titicaca

CHILE

FACTS ABOUT

PERU

63

Peru is located in South America. Peru is bordered on one side by the Pacific Ocean and the Amazon River flows through its rainforest region. The Andes Mountains and Colca Canyon, which is twice as deep as the Grand Canyon, are located in Peru. Llamas are animals that are used for travel through the Andes. The piranha is a deadly flesh-eating fish that lives in the Amazon River. The Incas, an ancient Indian tribe of Peru, were from the lost city of Machu Picchu.

CROSSWORD

401

Across

1. The river that flows through the rainforest region of Peru, otherwise known as the Selva.

2. The Colca Canyon in Peru is twice as deep as the famous _____ Canyon in the U.S.

Down

1. These animals are commonly used to carry packs and for travel through the difficult terrain of the Andes.

2. Machu Picchu is thought to be a lost city of this ancient Peruvian Indian tribe.

3. The _____ is a deadly flesh-eating fish that lives in the Amazon River.

4. The mountain range that makes up the sierra region of Peru is called the _____.

Make a Model of the Solar System: Uranus

Adult supervision is recommended.

Materials

$2\frac{1}{2}$" (6.4 cm) foam ball
10" (25.4 cm) piece of medium-gauge wire
ruler
blue acrylic (water-based) paint
white acrylic (water-based) paint
paintbrush
craft glue
scissors
old newspapers
model from the previous activity
play putty or modeling clay
toothpick

Uranus is the seventh planet from the sun. It is four times larger than Earth. The surface of Uranus has craters and frozen water. Like the Earth, Uranus experiences four seasons, but the temperature can get as cold as -364 degrees Fahrenheit (-220 degrees Celsius). The *Voyager 2* spacecraft took pictures of Uranus that show rings around the planet like those around Saturn. The rings of Uranus are flat and hard to see, even with a telescope.

Directions

1. Cover a table with newspapers.
2. Push a toothpick into the foam ball.

Uranus

3. Hold the foam ball by the toothpick, and paint the entire ball with light blue paint. You can make light blue by mixing a tiny bit of white paint with blue paint.

4. Gently push the toothpick into putty or modeling clay so the ball will dry without touching anything. Place the painted ball on a clean spot on the newspaper.

5. Let the ball dry for about five hours.

6. Cut out the Uranus label on the previous page, and glue it to the dried Uranus planet.

7. Measure the wire so that it is 10" (25.4 cm) long. Have an adult break or cut the wire to the correct length.

8. Put glue on one end of the wire. Push the wire about $\frac{1}{2}$" (1.3 cm) into the Uranus planet.

9. Put glue on the other end of the wire. Push 1" (2.5 cm) of the wire attached to the Uranus planet into the sun model about $2\frac{1}{2}$" (6.4 cm) from the Saturn wire.

Extension

William Herschel, an astronomer who lived in England, discovered Uranus in 1781. Imagine that you are William Herschel. On the lines below, write a journal entry from Herschel's point of view about his discovery.

_____

_____

_____

_____

_____

_____

_____

_____

All Aboard the Space Pod

Chapter 9

Addison and Luke stared at each other when they got back on the Space Pod. "That was close," said Luke, trying to catch his breath. Luke looked down and then let out a loud yell.

"What's the matter, Luke?" Addison asked in a worried voice.

"I dropped the ice sample," said Luke miserably. He still had a long face when D.I.D.G.E.T. reported their progress.

"We are approaching a planet that is 11 times larger than Earth," D.I.D.G.E.T. said.

"Let's see. This is our fifth planet. My very educated mother just…Jupiter," announced Addison.

Activity 1

Skill: Reading Comprehension

Answer the following questions on the lines provided.

1. Why was Luke out of breath?

   _____

2. Why was Luke miserable?

   _____

3. How did Addison react to Luke's yell?

   _____

"We are 600,000 miles away from Jupiter, and it still fills our viewing window!" Addison exclaimed.

Luke forgot that he was upset as he and Addison stared out the window.

D.I.D.G.E.T. shared his latest fact. "Jupiter is made mostly of gas."

"That's right," said Addison when Luke looked surprised. "Do you see that big, dark spot? It's just swirling gas. It's called the Great Red Spot. Some people think it's a gas hurricane that has lasted for 400 years."

The Space Pod jerked.

D.I.D.G.E.T. reported, "Jupiter's magnetic pull is 14 times stronger than Earth's. We should move on before we get pulled too close to get away."

Activity 2

Skill: Verbs

Verbs show action and make your writing clear and vivid. Vivid verbs allow writers to describe the same action in several different ways. Choose a vivid verb from the box to describe each action phrase.

dashed	whispered	hopped	strolled

1. said quietly _____

2. moved up and down _____

3. walked in a relaxed way _____

4. ran for a short distance _____

Antonyms, Synonyms and Homonyms

Antonyms are words that mean the opposite. Synonyms are words that mean the same. Homonyms are words that sound alike but mean something different. Circle antonym, synonym or homonym for each word group below.

1. happy   glad   ANTONYM • SYNONYM • HOMONYM

2. write   right   ANTONYM • SYNONYM • HOMONYM

3. black   white   ANTONYM • SYNONYM • HOMONYM

4. tall   short   ANTONYM • SYNONYM • HOMONYM

5. angry   mad   ANTONYM • SYNONYM • HOMONYM

6. see   sea   ANTONYM • SYNONYM • HOMONYM

Factoid

The Andes have more people living in them than any other mountain range in the world. The highest home in the world is a shepherd's hut in the Andes at 17,000 ft. (5180 m.).

Safety Tip

Electricity and water do not mix! Make sure that you do not use electrical appliances around water. Be especially careful with the hair dryer. Do not use it while you have water in the bathtub, sink, or a puddle on the floor. Always unplug small appliances when you are finished using them.

Can you find...?

Circle the items hidden in the picture.

Beaker

Microscope

Flask

Addison

D.I.D.G.E.T.

Math C.O.D.E.D = Messages

At 22,205 ft. (6,765 meters), this mountain is the highest mountain in Peru.

11 + 4	35 - 29	32 - 16	9 + 3	20 - 7	11+ 5	27 - 19	41 - 25	56 - 52

1 = o	6 = u	11 = l	16 = a
2 = m	7 = q	12 = s	17 = d
3 = y	8 = r	13 = c	
4 = n	9 = t	14 = p	
5 = e	10 = i	15 = h	

FRIDAY

I feel _____ today because...

_____

_____

_____

_____

_____

_____

_____

_____

_____

_____

MAZE

START

END

Can you get the facts straight? Choose from these words to complete the story! Beware, there are extra words to make it more challenging!

mountains	learn	believed	stared
helping	song	Andes	looked
humming	flute	spooky	mummies
travel	preserved	llamas	

Children of the Sun

Addison _____ at the picture of Machu Picchu. It _____ like
                    verb   verb
a mountain castle, but she knew it was a whole ancient Inca city. She caught

herself _____. D.I.D.G.E.T. was playing music.
              verb

"What's that, D.I.D.G.E.T.? It's _____—like it comes from outer
                                      adjective
space."

"No—from Peru. It goes with your picture," D.I.D.G.E.T. signaled. "It's

Incan music. We know the English words:

I am a son of the Sun, going to those of my race.

I'm one of the children of the Sun, going to my people.

I'm a child of the Sun, coming for a purpose."

"That's a funny thing for a kid to sing," Addison thought. "Purpose usually

means something big and important." She looked at the rest of D.I.D.G.E.T.'s

message.

The Inca _____ the mountains were their gods. The song is about
              verb
children who were sacrificed—left on the mountains—for the gods. "Oh,

that's terrible, D.I.D.G.E.T.!" she cried.

She read more. The children weren't frightened. They thought what they

were doing was special. They believed they were _____ their whole
                                                        verb
world. They did, too. It's very cold in the _____, and the children froze
                                                  noun
into "ice _____." They look now just as they did then. We can see how
              noun
they dressed. We can tell what they ate. What they did _____ their
                                                              verb
whole world for us to _____ about today.

"That **is** special," said Addison.
                         verb

(125)

activity

Adult supervision is recommended.

Twine and Clay Pot

Directions:

❶ Put a line of glue around the top of the pot under the top lip.

❷ Start winding twine around the pot and in the glue.

❸ Add more glue and keep winding the twine around the pot until it is covered. Be sure there is no space between the lines of twine.

❹ Cut off the twine and put a dot of glue on the end of it.

❺ Press the end down smoothly so it blends in with the other twine.

❻ Let the pot dry completely before using it.

Materials:

clay pot
twine or jute
craft glue
scissors

PLACE VALUES

Write the correct number or fill in the correct amount of marks in each place.

Example:

1000s	100s	10s	1s
/	####///	//	////

Answer: 1,824

1.

1000s	100s	10s	1s
////	////	####//	////

_____

2.

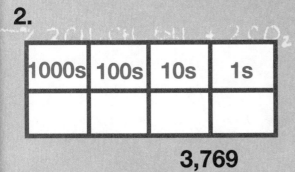

1000s	100s	10s	1s

3,769

3.

1000s	100s	10s	1s
####/	####	####	####

_____

4.

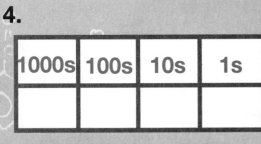

1000s	100s	10s	1s

2,436

5.

1000s	100s	10s	1s
////	//	####/	///

_____

6.

1000s	100s	10s	1s

7,392

7.

1000s	100s	10s	1s
####///	####/////	/	####/

_____

8.

1000s	100s	10s	1s

5,637

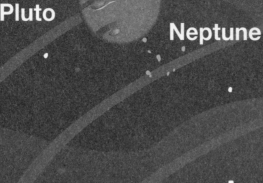

Pluto

Neptune

Jupiter

Uranus

Solar System
Facts

Sun

- The sun is at the center of the solar system.
- The sun is a yellow star.
- All the planets revolve around the sun.

Mercury

- Mercury is closest to the sun.
- Second smallest planet in the solar system.
- Average temperature ranges from –297.4 degrees Fahrenheit (–183 degrees Celcius) to 800 degrees Fahrenheit (427 degrees Celcius) in one day.

Venus

- Second planet from the sun.
- Venus is Earth's closest neighbor, 25 million miles away.
- Venus is the hottest planet in the solar system. Its surface can get as hot as 900 degrees Fahrenheit (484 degrees Celcius).

Earth

- Third planet from the sun.
- 70 percent of the earth's surface is covered with water.
- Earth's highest point is Mt. Everest – 29,035 ft. (8,850 m.).

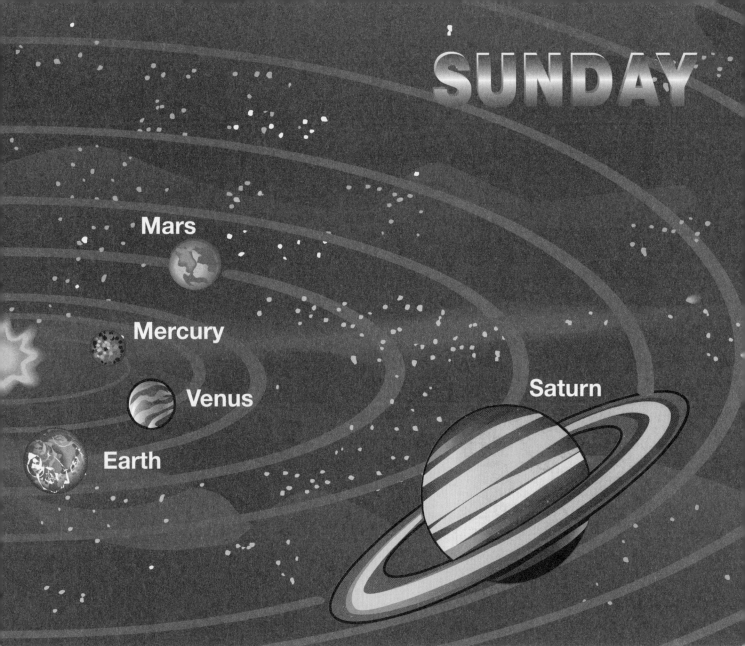

Mars

Mercury

Venus

Earth

Saturn

Crossword

Across

1. Highest point on Earth.

2. All the planets _____ around the sun.

3. 70 percent of the Earth's surface is covered with this.

4. The sun is a yellow _____.

Down

1. Where the sun is located in the solar system.

2. Planet closest to the sun.

3. Earth's closest neighbor.

4. Third planet from the sun.

SAUDI
ARABIA

FACTS ABOUT
SAUDI ARABIA

Saudi Arabia is the largest kingdom in Asia. It is bordered by the Red Sea on one side and the Persian Gulf on the other. Most of Saudi Arabia is a vast desert. In the desert, an oasis is a place where underground water reaches the surface allowing crops and palm trees to grow. Camels are animals that live in the desert. They are known as "ships of the desert" and can go for weeks without water. Saudi Arabia is a wealthy country because they have an abundance of oil to sell to other countries.

63

CROSSWORD

Across

1. Saudi Arabia is a wealthy country because they have an abundance of this valuable natural resource which they sell to other countries.

2. Saudi Arabia is bordered by the Red Sea on one side and the _____ Gulf on the other.

3. Saudi Arabia is the largest kingdom on this continent.

Down

1. Most of Saudi Arabia is a vast _____.

2. An _____ is a place where underground water reaches the surface allowing crops and palm trees to grow in the desert.

3. These animals are known as the "ships of the desert." They can go for weeks without water.

Make a Model of the Solar System: Neptune

Adult supervision is recommended.

Materials

2 $\frac{1}{2}$" (6.4 cm) foam ball
11 $\frac{1}{2}$" (29.2 cm) piece of medium-gauge wire
ruler
blue acrylic (water-based) paint
black acrylic (water-based) paint
paintbrush
craft glue
scissors
old newspapers
model from the previous activity
play putty or modeling clay
toothpick

Neptune is the eighth planet from the sun—most of the time! From 1979 to 1999 Neptune was the farthest planet from the sun. Every 248 years Neptune is the farthest planet from the sun because Pluto orbits closer to the sun during this time. Neptune is so large that, if it were hollow, 60 Earths could fit inside it! The average temperature of Neptune is very cold: -274 degrees Fahrenheit (-170 degrees Celsius).

Directions

1. Spread clean newspapers over a table.
2. Push a toothpick into the foam ball.

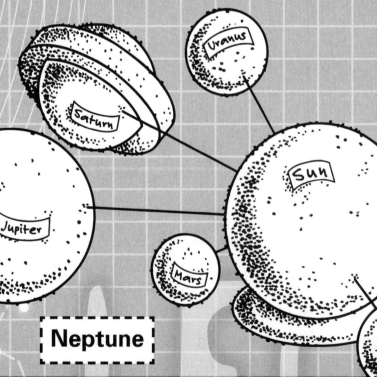

Neptune

3. Hold the foam ball by the toothpick, and paint the entire ball with dark blue paint. You can make dark blue by mixing a tiny bit of black with blue paint.

4. Gently push the toothpick into putty or modeling clay so the ball will dry without touching anything. Place the painted ball on a clean spot on the newspaper.

5. Let the ball dry for about five hours.

6. Cut out the Neptune label on the previous page, and glue it to the dried Neptune planet model.

7. Measure the wire so that it is $11\frac{1}{2}$" (29.2 cm) long. Have an adult break or cut the wire to the correct length.

8. Put glue on one end of the wire. Push the wire about $\frac{1}{2}$" (1.3 cm) into the Neptune planet.

9. Put glue on the other end of the wire. Push 1" (2.5 cm) of the wire attached to Neptune into the sun model about $1\frac{3}{4}$" (4.5 cm) from the Uranus wire.

Extension

What do Jupiter, Saturn, Uranus and Neptune have in common? They are all made of gases, meaning that they aren't solid or liquid. Learn more about these gas planets at your local library. Then on the lines below, compare and contrast these four planets.

_____

_____

_____

_____

_____

_____

_____

All Aboard the Space Pod

Chapter 10

The Space Pod moved to avoid Jupiter's strong magnetic pull. Addison floated and flipped over to a locked cabinet. When she floated back, she handed Luke a pair of dark glasses.

"What are these for?" Luke asked.

"These glasses will help you see the special features of the next three gas planets—Saturn, Uranus and Neptune," said Addison.

"Look at Saturn's rings, Add. They look like those neon necklaces we get from the fair that glow in the dark," Luke observed.

"Look at the pattern of stripes the clouds form around Saturn," Addison pointed out.

The Space Pod moved closer to Uranus.

Activity 1

Skill: Creative Writing

Write a journal entry from Luke, in which he describes his journey. Use this sentence to begin your entry:

When Addison first showed me the Space Pod, I couldn't believe my eyes. _____

_____

_____

_____

_____

_____

"The gas that gives Uranus its blue-green color is methane. Uranus also has the largest number of moons of any of the planets," D.I.D.G.E.T. said.

"Luke, use your glasses and see how many moons you can count," Addison instructed.

"I see 17," Luke counted.

"Do you notice anything different about Uranus?" Addison quizzed Luke.

Luke looked through his glasses and shook his head no.

"If we were looking at Uranus from Earth, we would see that it rotates differently from most other planets. Instead of rotating from side to side, Uranus rotates from top to bottom," Addison reported.

"Some astronomers believe that Uranus was knocked on its side," D.I.D.G.E.T. added.

Activity 2

Skill: Creative Writing

What special instrument would you invent for space travel? Draw and label a diagram, or write a description of your invention. Be sure to show or tell what your invention is and how it works.

SPELLING QUIZ

Listed below is a group of words that represent things shown in the picture on page 137. Circle the correct spelling for each word.

1. pawlm tree   palm tree
2. clouds   clowds
3. sheap   sheep
4. bilding   building
5. kar   car
6. camel   camle
7. shyp   ship
8. sand   sande

Factoid

The Rub-Al-Khali or the "Empty Quarter" is the largest desert in the world. It covers more than 250,000 square miles. That's about the size of the state of Texas.

Safety Tip

Swimming is fun. But be safe! Swimming safety is very important. Never go near water, like a lake, canal or pool without an adult watching. If you are not an excellent swimmer, wear safety floating gear, even in shallow water. It is also best to swim with a friend in case one of you needs help. Swimming is fun, and if you need to learn, ask to be enrolled in a swimming class.

Can you find...?

Circle the items hidden in the picture.

Beaker

Microscope

Flask

Addison

D.I.D.G.E.T.

Math CODED Messages

$C O D E D$
$= -+$

These nomadic people roamed Saudi Arabia in search of pasture for their animals and lived in tents.

‾‾‾‾ ‾‾‾ ‾‾‾‾ ‾‾‾‾ ‾‾‾‾ ‾‾‾‾ ‾‾‾ ‾‾‾‾
53 - 43 6 + 3 35 - 27 11 + 2 51 - 39 24 - 19 9 + 2 28 - 21

1 = f	6 = t	11 = n
2 = p	7 = s	12 = u
3 = g	8 = d	13 = o
4 = y	9 = e	
5 = i	10 = b	

I feel _____ today because...

_____

_____

_____

_____

_____

_____

_____

_____

_____

_____

MAZE

END

START

Can you get the facts straight? Choose from these words to complete the story! Beware, there are extra words to make it more challenging!

sun	**sand**	**eyelashes**	**desert**
camel	**attic**	**oasis**	**oil**
carry	**spit**	**tent**	**feet**
water	**many**	**like**	

One Hump or Two?

"Addison's been in the _____ again," laughed her mother.

noun

Addison had a statue of a _____ in her hand. "Do these really spit

noun

tobacco juice?" she asked.

"Well, they _____ something," her mother answered. "They're

verb

moody, but they are one of the most useful animals in the world."

"Useful? You mean people still ride these things?"

"Yes, ride them and use them to _____ things, and even race

verb

them," said her mother. "Ask D.I.D.G.E.T."

"Well?" Addison punched D.I.D.G.E.T.'s query button. "Do they ride

camels anyplace that isn't some kind of museum?"

D.I.D.G.E.T. beeped a great many beeps. "People use camels almost

every place there is a _____. Camels have broad _____ that let

noun / noun

them travel on hot, loose _____. They can go several days without

noun

water and _____ days without food."

adjective

"Oh, I like this," Addison laughed. D.I.D.G.E.T. had printed, "Camels

have really beautiful long _____ to protect their eyes from the sun."

noun

"Even modern and oil-rich countries like Saudi Arabia still use these guys

out in the desert, huh?" Addison looked at the little statue again.

This time D.I.D.G.E.T. beeped a big "No." Addison's little camel had long

hair and two humps on its back. That made it a Bactrian camel from the cold

Gobi Desert. In hot deserts like the Arabian Desert, camels were

Dromedaries, with just one hump.

"I _____ you anyway," said Addison, giving the statue a pat.

verb

Adult supervision is recommended.

Materials:

colored chalk

black construction
  paper

masking tape

sheet of newspaper

aerosol hair spray

Chalk Art

Directions:

❶ This project is a little messy. Lay the black construction paper on a sheet of newspaper.

❷ Place several strips of masking tape in a pleasing design across the black paper as shown.

❸ Rub colored chalk on all the black open spaces left on the paper.

❹ Carefully remove the tape, one strip at a time, starting with the last strip that was put on.

❺ There will be a black line where the tape was attached.

❻ Lightly spray the finished picture with hair spray to keep the chalk from coming off.

MULTIPLICATION

Multiplication is a short way to find the sum of adding the same number a certain amount of times.

Any number x 1 = the number. Example: $1 \times 5 = 5$

$$1 + 1 + 1 + 1 + 1 = 5$$

Complete the multiplication problems below:

1. 1 x 10 =

2. 1 x 1 =

3. 1 x 9 =

4. 1 x 7 =

5. 1 x 8 =

6. 1 x 14 =

7. 1 x 99 =

8. 1 x 17 =

9. 1 x 24 =

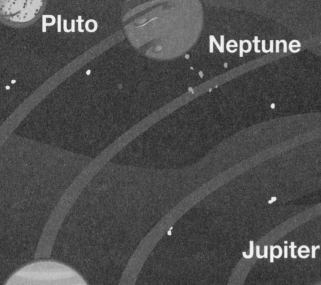

Pluto

Neptune

Jupiter

Uranus

Solar System Facts

Mars

- Fourth planet from the sun.
- Has the largest volcano and canyon in the solar system.
- Reddish in color because of the iron in the soil.

Jupiter

- Fifth planet from the sun.
- Largest planet in the solar system—all of the other planets could fit inside it together.
- Has 16 moons.

Saturn

- Sixth planet from the sun.
- Has rings that are made up of ice and rock particles. The particles can be as small as pebbles and as large as a house.
- Saturn's average temperature is –301.27 degrees Fahrenheit (–185.15 degrees Celcius.)

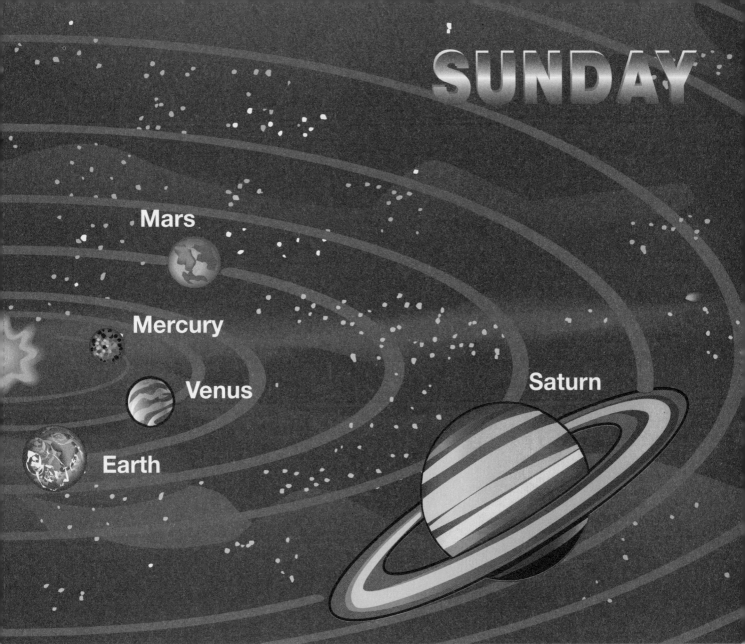

Mars

Mercury

Venus

Saturn

Earth

Crossword

Across

1. Largest planet in the solar system.
2. Number of moons that Jupiter has.
3. Saturn is the _____ planet from the sun.

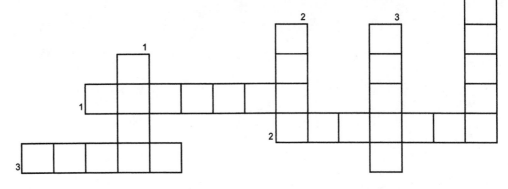

Down

1. Mars is reddish in color because of the ____ in its soil.

2. Has the largest volcano and canyon in the solar system.
3. Jupiter is the ____ planet from the sun.
4. Planet with rings.

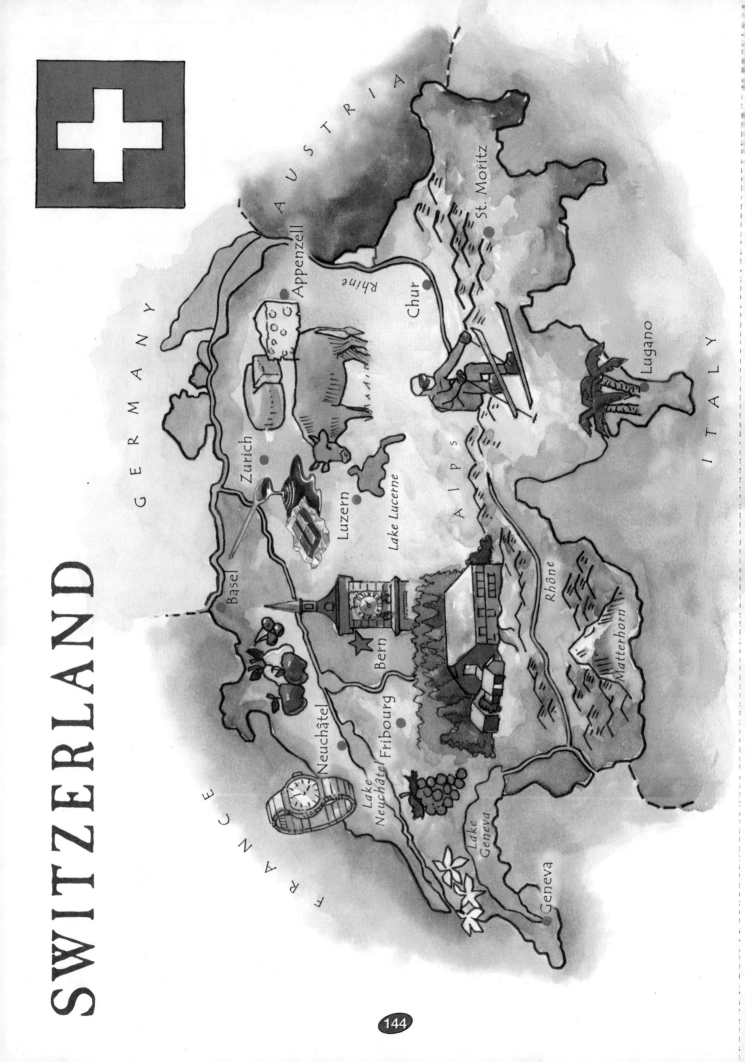

SWITZERLAND

GERMANY

AUSTRIA

FRANCE

ITALY

Appenzell

Rhine

St. Moritz

Chur

Lugano

Zurich

Basel

Luzern

Lake Lucerne

Alps

Bern

Neuchâtel

Lake Neuchâtel

Fribourg

Rhône

Matterhorn

Lake Geneva

Geneva

FACTS ABOUT
SWITZERLAND

Switzerland is located in Central Europe. There are three languages spoken there—German in the north, central, and eastern portion, French in the West, and Italian in the South. The Swiss Alps cover about 60 percent of Switzerland. People travel from all over Europe to ski there. The Swiss are famous for chocolate and fondue, a dish in which meat or bread is placed on skewers and dipped into a pot of melted cheese or boiling oil. The Swiss flag is red with a white cross in the center.

63

CROSSWORD

401

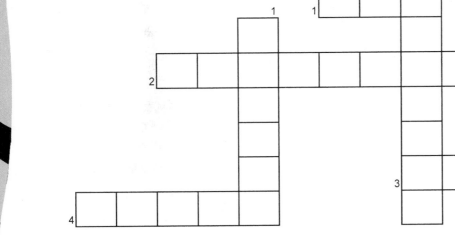

Across

1. People travel from all over Europe to _____ in the Swiss Alps.

2. The Swiss are famous for this smooth brown sweet.

3. This mountain range covers about 60 percent of Switzerland.

4. The Swiss flag is red with a _____ cross in the center.

Down

1. A Swiss dish in which meat or bread is placed on skewers and dipped into a pot of melted cheese or boiling oil.

2. This language is spoken in the southern part of Switzerland.

Make a Model of the Solar System: Pluto

Adult supervision is recommended.

Materials

1" (2.5 cm) foam ball
14" (35.6 cm) piece of medium-gauge wire
ruler
purple acrylic (water-based) paint, or
  red acrylic (water-based) paint and
  blue acrylic (water-based) paint
paintbrush
craft glue
scissors
old newspapers
model from the previous activity
play putty or modeling clay
toothpick

Pluto is the smallest and coldest planet in our solar system. It is about six times smaller than Earth and is made of rock and ice. The average temperature on Pluto is -333.67 degrees Fahrenheit (-203.15 degrees Celsius). It takes Pluto almost 248 Earth years to travel around the sun! Pluto has one known moon, called Charon, which is half the size of Pluto. Some astronomers call Pluto and Charon a double planet.

Directions

1. Cover a table with newspapers.
2. Push a toothpick into the foam ball.

Pluto

3. Hold the foam ball by the toothpick, and paint the entire ball with purple paint. If you do not have purple paint, mix red and blue paint together.

4. Gently push the toothpick into putty or modeling clay so the ball will dry without touching anything. Place the painted ball on a clean spot on the newspaper.

5. Let the ball dry for about five hours.

6. Cut out the Pluto label on the previous page, and glue it to the dried Pluto planet model.

7. Measure the wire so that it is 14" (35.6 cm) long. Have an adult break or cut the wire to the correct length.

8. Put glue on one end of the wire. Push the wire about $\frac{1}{2}$" (1.3 cm) into the Pluto planet.

9. Put glue on the other end of the wire. Push 1" (2.5 cm) of the wire attached to Pluto into the sun model about 2" (5.1 cm) from the Neptune wire.

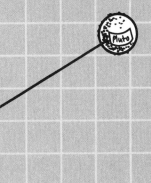

Extension

Pluto is the only planet that has never been visited by a spacecraft from Earth. Learn more about Pluto at your local library. Then, imagine that you are part of the first space mission to Pluto. On the lines below, write a story about your experiences.

_____

_____

_____

_____

_____

_____

_____

All Aboard the Space Pod

Chapter 11

Luke liked the details that the glasses helped him see.

"What you see moving into our view now is Neptune," D.I.D.G.E.T. announced.

"Luke, did you know that life may have existed on Neptune?" Addison asked.

"Alien kind of life?" Luke questioned.

"No, silly. More like plant life or tiny, tiny organisms," Addison responded. "Scientists are still researching to determine what type of life existed and why it is no longer there."

Activity 1

Skill: Character Sketch

Complete the chart below. In the right column, use words or phrases to describe Addison, Luke and D.I.D.G.E.T.

Character Name	Character Description
Addison	
Luke	
D.I.D.G.E.T.	

"What about Pluto?" Luke asked as the pod moved past Neptune.

"Not much is known about Pluto. Pluto is the only planet that has not been visited by a space mission," Addison responded.

"Maybe you could be the first to find out more, Addison," Luke suggested.

The pod started to shake and spin. Addison grabbed Luke and pulled him to his seat. After much struggle, they were belted in.

"Pluto rotates in the opposite direction from most other planets. We must remove ourselves from Pluto's path," D.I.D.G.E.T. warned.

Addison punched the new course into the control pad. Destination—Earth!

Activity 2

Skill: Reading Comprehension

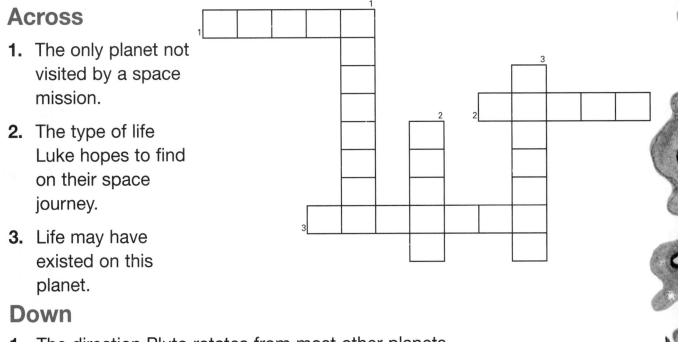

Across

1. The only planet not visited by a space mission.

2. The type of life Luke hopes to find on their space journey.

3. Life may have existed on this planet.

Down

1. The direction Pluto rotates from most other planets

2. Addison, Luke, and D.I.D.G.E.T.'s final destination.

3. One of Addison's inventions that helped Luke view the gas planets.

SILENT LETTERS

Many words have silent letters. Example: ans(w)er
Circle the silent letters in each word below.

1. knife

2. wrap

3. scent

4. comb

5. wrong

6. straight

7. hour

8. high

Factoid

Switzerland is a peaceful country that is considered neutral. That means that in an international conflict, Switzerland will not take sides.

Safety Tip

Most animals are friendly, but remember that not all animals are friendly. If a dog is growling and barking at you, keep your distance. It could mean that he does not want you to play with him. Other creatures like snakes and spiders can be dangerous as well, so don't go near any animals you do not know.

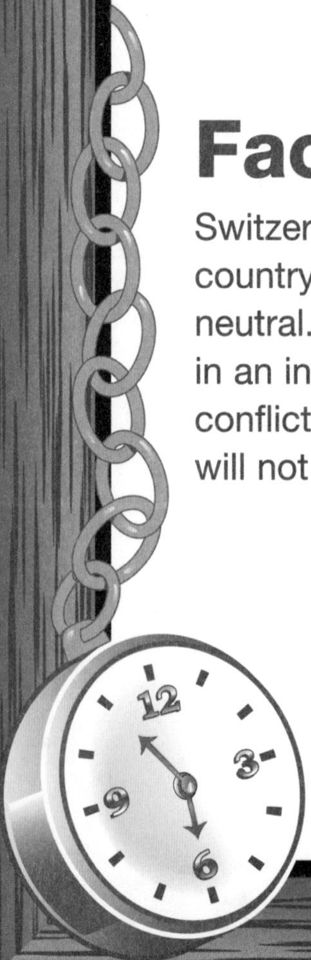

Can you find...?

Circle the items hidden in the picture.

Beaker

Microscope

Flask

Addison

D.I.D.G.E.T.

Math CODED Messages

Highly praised for their craftsmanship, Swiss watches are made in this city.

$\overline{}$ $\overline{}$ $\overline{}$ $\overline{}$ $\overline{}$ $\overline{}$ $\overline{}$ $\overline{}$ $\overline{}$
42 - 32 12 + 4 29 - 15 42 - 27 4 + 7 16 - 4 2 + 7 25 - 13 39 - 26

1 = j	5 = f	9 = t	13 = l
2 = k	6 = y	10 = n	14 = u
3 = m	7 = o	11 = h	15 = c
4 = b	8 = g	12 = a	16 = e

I feel _____ today because...

_____

_____

_____

_____

_____

_____

_____

_____

_____

MAZE

END

START

Can you get the facts straight? Choose from these words to complete the story! Beware, there are extra words to make it more challenging!

cheese   page   grass   wobbly   yodel
hiking   airplane   turned   trail   reading
blue   music   speaking   picture   orange

Picture Perfect

Addison and her friend Tommy were _____ a travel magazine.
                 verb
"Look at that picture. It's got to be fake. No sky is that _____,"
                 adjective
said Addison.

"Yeah," Tommy answered. "Those mountains look like they came

out of a storybook."

"Wait!" Addison had seen something else in the picture. "Those are

hang gliders, and it looks like real people _____ along that _____."
           verb   noun

"Turn the _____, and let's see what it says!" said Tommy.
        noun

The next page held another beautiful _____—this time of a girl
                 noun
about Addison's age. She was sitting in the middle of a field. The

_____ around her was tall and very green. She was trying to pick
noun
flowers, but a _____ baby goat was in her way. Maybe he was trying
       adjective
to help! There were other goats eating grass there, too. Far away,

Addison could see the same tall, pointed mountains that were in the

first picture. Across the bottom of the page she read, "A modern Heidi

plays with her friends."

"Who's Heidi?" asked Tommy.

"She's a girl in a storybook," replied Addison. "She lived in…"

Tommy _____ the page before Addison finished _____. "Come
       verb   verb
to beautiful…," he read.

"SWITZERLAND!" he and Addison said at the same time.

activity

Adult supervision is recommended.

Sunshine Picture

Directions:

1. Cut a circle and some triangles from aluminum foil.

2. Arrange them shiny-side up on the construction paper to form a sun.

3. Glue the aluminum foil in place.

4. Take the picture outside on a sunny day and watch the sunlight bounce off it.

Materials:

aluminum foil

black or purple construction paper

scissors

non-toxic white glue

MULTIPLICATION

Multiplication is a short way to find the sum of adding the same number a certain amount of times.

Any number x 2 = the number + itself. Example: 4 x 2 = 8

4 + 4 = 8

Complete the multiplication problems below:

1.   1 x 2 =

(1 + 1)

2.   5 x 2 =

(5 + 5)

3.   3 x 2 =

(3 + 3)

4.   7 x 2 =

(7 + 7)

5.   10 x 2 =

(10 + 10)

6.   8 x 2 =

(8 + 8)

7.   6 x 2 =

(6 + 6)

8.   2 x 2 =

(2 + 2)

9.   9 x 2 =

(9 + 9)

Pluto

Neptune

Jupiter

Uranus

Solar System **Facts**

Uranus

- Seventh planet from the sun.
- Blue-green in color.
- Also has rings around it, but they aren't as large as Saturn's rings so they are hard to see.

Neptune

- Eighth planet from the sun.
- Takes 165 Earth-years to revolve around the sun one time.
- The average temperature of Neptune is very cold: -274 degrees Fahrenheit (-170 degrees Celsius).

Pluto

- Ninth and farthest planet from the sun—3.6 billion miles away.
- Smallest planet in solar system.
- Takes 248 Earth-years to revolve around the sun one time.

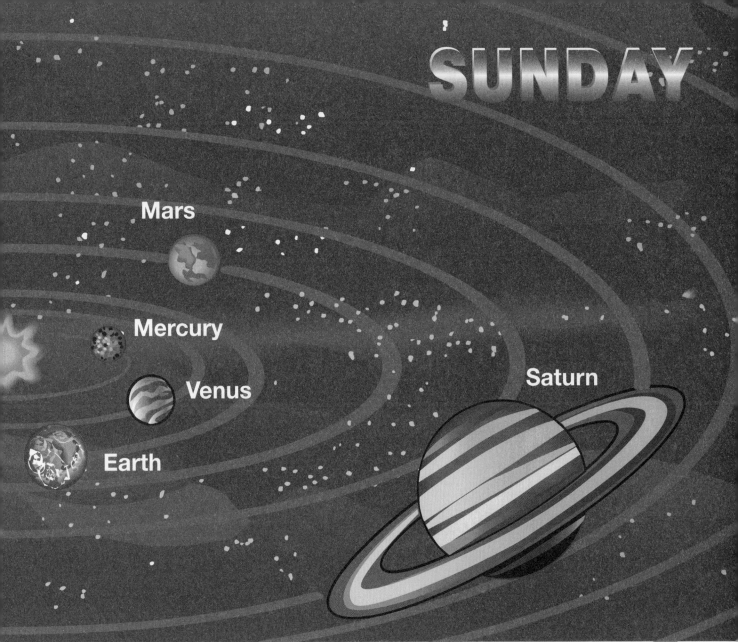

Crossword

Across

1. Color of Uranus.

2. Pluto is the _____ planet in the solar system.

3. Uranus has _____ that aren't as big as the ones around Saturn.

4. Planet with the average temperature of -274 degrees Fahrenheit (-170 degrees Celsius).

Down

1. Farthest planet from the sun.

2. Seventh planet from the sun.

3. Pluto takes 248 Earth-years to revolve around the _____ one time.

4. Pluto is 3.6 _____ miles away from the sun.

157

UNITED STATES

ATLANTIC OCEAN

PACIFIC OCEAN

CANADA

MEXICO

GULF OF MEXICO

MAINE
Augusta
NEW HAMPSHIRE
VERMONT
Concord
Montpelier
MASSACHUSETTS
RHODE ISLAND
CONNECTICUT
Boston
Providence
Hartford
Albany
NEW YORK
Lake Ontario
Buffalo
Lake Erie
NEW JERSEY
Trenton
Dover
DELAWARE
MARYLAND
Annapolis
PENNSYLVANIA
Harrisburg
Philadelphia
WASHINGTON D.C.
Richmond
VIRGINIA
WEST VIRGINIA
Charleston
Raleigh
NORTH CAROLINA
Columbia
SOUTH CAROLINA
Savannah
GEORGIA
Atlanta
Tallahassee
FLORIDA
Orlando
Miami

OHIO
Columbus
Cincinnati
Frankfort
KENTUCKY
Ohio River
Nashville
TENNESSEE
ALABAMA
Birmingham
Montgomery
MISSISSIPPI
Jackson
New Orleans

INDIANA
Indianapolis
ILLINOIS
Springfield
St. Louis
MISSOURI
Jefferson City
ARKANSAS
Little Rock
Mississippi River
Baton Rouge
LOUISIANA

MICHIGAN
Lansing
Detroit
Lake Huron
Lake Michigan
WISCONSIN
Madison
Milwaukee
Chicago
Lake Superior

MINNESOTA
St. Paul
Minneapolis
IOWA
Des Moines
NEBRASKA
Lincoln
Topeka
KANSAS
OKLAHOMA
Oklahoma City
Tulsa
Fort Worth
TEXAS
Austin
Houston
Rio Grande

NORTH DAKOTA
Bismarck
SOUTH DAKOTA
Pierre
Missouri River
WYOMING
Cheyenne
Denver
COLORADO
Santa Fe
NEW MEXICO

MONTANA
Helena
IDAHO
Boise
UTAH
Salt Lake City
Colorado River
ARIZONA
Phoenix

WASHINGTON
Olympia
Seattle
Columbia
OREGON
Salem
Salt Lake City
NEVADA
Carson City
CALIFORNIA
Sacramento
San Francisco
Las Vegas
Los Angeles

HAWAII
Honolulu

ALASKA
Juneau

MONDAY

USA

The United States of America is located in North America. Tribes of American Indians were living in America before the Europeans settled the "New World." The Civil War was a war fought between the northern and southern states from 1861 to 1865. The Statue of Liberty and Mt. Rushmore are famous tourist attractions. The Statue of Liberty is located in New York City's harbor. Mt. Rushmore is located in South Dakota. Mt. McKinley, located in Alaska, is the highest peak in all of North America. Lake Superior, which borders Michigan, Wisconsin, Minnesota and Ontario, is the largest freshwater lake in the world.

63

CROSSWORD

Across

1. The _____ War was a war fought between the northern and southern states from 1861 to 1865.

2. Mt. _____ features the faces of George Washington, Thomas Jefferson, Theodore Roosevelt and Abraham Lincoln carved into the Black Hills in South Dakota.

Down

1. The largest freshwater lake in the world. It borders Michigan, Wisconsin, and Minnesota in the U.S. and Ontario in Canada.

2. Mt. McKinley in this state is the highest peak in all of North America.

3. The Statue of _____ in New York City's harbor was the first glimpse of a new world for early immigrants who came to the U.S. by ship.

4. Tribes of American _____ such as the Apache, Navajo and Sioux were all living in America long before Europeans arrived to settle in the "New World."

Make a Model of the Solar System: Your Solar System

Adult supervision is recommended.

Materials

glitter spray paint (make sure
  it can be used on foam)

old newspapers

completed model from
  the previous activity

> Our solar system is a unique and awesome place! Besides planets, it has stars, *comets* (frozen masses of dust and gas), *asteroids* (rocky objects), and *meteors* (small particles of rock and dust).

Directions

1. Spread clean newspapers outside, away from any objects or people. Make sure the wind is not blowing.

2. Place the model on the newspapers.

3. Shake the paint can and *lightly* spray the planets with the glitter paint.

4. Display your finished solar system on a table or shelf.

Extension

Using the letters of each planet, write a fact about the planet on the lines below. For example, you might write the following for Mars: M—Mighty rocky, A—All rich in iron, R—Red color, S—Shiver in cold. Use another sheet of paper if necessary.

_____

_____

_____

_____

_____

Congratulations on finishing your solar system model! Now, as you begin third grade, you can name the planets and share neat facts about our solar system with your class.

All Aboard the Space Pod

Chapter 12

The Space Pod began to head back to Earth. Special shields came down over the windows to protect the pod from the heat of re-entering Earth's atmosphere. It was weird not to be able to see out the windows. Luke didn't like it.

"Just another 14 seconds," reassured D.I.D.G.E.T.

Luke held his breath. "Four . . . three . . . two . . . one!" he counted in his head. Slowly he opened his eyes and let go of his sister's hand.

Activity 1

Skill: Story Comprehension

Answer the following questions on the lines provided.

1. On what planet(s) does the Space Pod land and explore?

_____

2. Name the gas planets.

_____

3. Why do special shields come down over the windows?

_____

4. What is the pod's final destination?

_____

5. What is D.I.D.G.E.T.'s role in the story?

_____

"Hooray!" cheered Luke and Addison together. The shields were gone.

"Have you ever seen a prettier sight?" asked Addison. Luke shook his head.

"Water and solid ground and clouds," listed Luke. "Do you think we can land on this planet?" he teased.

"We will land in 1.5 minutes," D.I.D.G.E.T. announced.

Luke counted to 90. Thump! "Sure enough, D.I.D.G.E.T., you were right," Luke said with a grin.

"And there's another pretty sight," said Addison, pointing toward the house. Luke looked where Addison was pointing. Their parents were walking down the hill toward the lab.

Activity 2

Skill: Sequence of Events

Number the events in the order in which they happened in the story.

_____ **1.** Earth is in sight.

_____ **2.** Shields cover the windows.

_____ **3.** The Space Pod lands.

_____ **4.** Luke and Addison see their parents.

_____ **5.** The children cheer.

_____ **6.** Luke counts backward.

FIVE SENSES

The five senses are 1) sight, 2) hearing, 3) taste, 4) touch, and 5) smell. Listed below are statements that relate to the picture on page 165. Circle the sense that would be used in each statement.

1. The lady with the blond hair squeezed the fruit to make sure it was fresh.

   sight   hearing   taste   touch   smell

2. The man with the hat was going home to eat a sandwich made with the freshly baked bread that he had bought.

   sight   hearing   taste   touch   smell

3. People stopped after the policeman blew his whistle.

   sight   hearing   taste   touch   smell

4. The exhaust from all the cars made a bad odor.

   sight   hearing   taste   touch   smell

5. The man looking out of the top window was shocked that the flowerpot was falling and would hit the man below on the head.

   sight   hearing   taste   touch   smell

Factoid

The U.S. bought the Louisiana Territory from France in 1803. A team of explorers—Meriwether Lewis and William Clark—were sent by Thomas Jefferson to chart the new territory which went all the way to the Pacific Ocean and doubled the size of the U.S. They had a Shoshone Indian woman named Sacajawea as a guide.

Safety Tip

Ride your bike or skateboard safely. Always wear a helmet and bright clothing when you ride your bike or skateboard. Always be aware of your surroundings and be ready to stop at any moment. Try not to ride at night. But if you do, make sure that you have reflective tape and lights that are visible. Also, when riding your skateboard, use elbow and knee pads.

Can you find...?

Circle the items hidden in the picture.

Beaker

Microscope

Flask

Addison

D.I.D.G.E.T.

Math
C O D E D
Messages

The United States is home to people of many countries. From 1892 to 1954, more than 12 million immigrants went here to receive permission to enter the U.S.

$$\overline{\text{29 - 24}} \quad \overline{\text{47 - 30}} \quad \overline{\text{8 + 9}} \quad \overline{\text{53 - 32}} \quad \overline{\text{14 - 2}}$$

$$\overline{\text{10 + 11}} \quad \overline{\text{48 - 36}} \quad \overline{\text{5 + 12}} \quad \overline{\text{39 - 24}} \quad \overline{\text{19 - 15}} \quad \overline{\text{46 - 26}}$$

1 = o	6 = u	11 = j	16 = h	21 = i
2 = m	7 = q	12 = s	17 = l	22 = w
3 = y	8 = g	13 = c	18 = f	
4 = n	9 = t	14 = p	19 = r	
5 = e	10 = b	15 = a	20 = d	

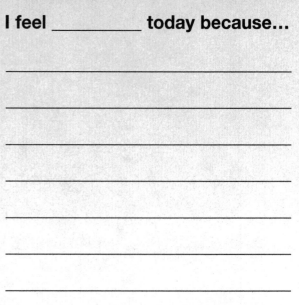

I feel _____ today because...

_____

_____

_____

_____

_____

_____

_____

_____

_____

_____

_____

MAZE

END

START

Can you get the facts straight? Choose from these words to complete the story! Beware, there are extra words to make it more challenging!

cheese	chicken	candy	flashed
plain	beeped	flagpole	happy
bored	disagreed	flag	clues
foods	cheered	box	

Eating American

"There's still one ——————
<small>noun</small>
to put away, Addison," said Tommy.

"I know," Addison groaned, "But it's no fun now because there's only one ——————— to choose from.
<small>noun</small>
The game's over."

"Let's read the ——————— on
<small>noun</small>
the box anyway."
Tommy grabbed the box lid.

"I know what it says." Addison sounded ———————. "It says 'The
<small>adjective</small>
Stars and Stripes' for the U.S. flag."

"It says something else, too,"
——————— Tommy. "It looks like
<small>verb</small>
someone was planning a Fourth of July picnic with all our favorite American ———————."
<small>noun</small>

"Really? What were they having?" asked Addison. "Maybe we can fix the same thing."

"Well, pizza, for starters," said Tommy.

"That's Italian. What else?" asked Addison.

"Hot dogs," read Tommy.

"German," said Addison.

"French fries."

"They're French, silly!" Addison laughed.

"Swiss and Cheddar ———————."
<small>noun</small>

"Switzerland and England," sighed Addison.

"Ice cream?" said Tommy hopefully.

Addison shook her head. "Italian."

"Lemonade?"

"They drink that in Arabia. Honestly, did they have anything at all that was ———————
<small>adjective</small>
old American?"

All of a sudden D.I.D.G.E.T. began to beep loudly. He even ———————
<small>verb</small>
his lights. Addison leaned over to look at D.I.D.G.E.T.'s display. "Gee, that's right," she said.

"What? What does he say?" asked Tommy.

D.I.D.G.E.T. ——————— again.
<small>verb</small>
"All of it is American," Addison read. "And so are all of us!"

activity

Adult supervision is recommended.

Magazine Message

Directions:

1. Write a message to someone you know.

2. Cut out words from magazines or newspapers.

3. Arrange them on paper to make a message.

4. Glue the words in place.

5. Mail the message.

Materials:

old magazines or
  newspapers

non-toxic white glue

plain paper

scissors

COUNTING MONEY

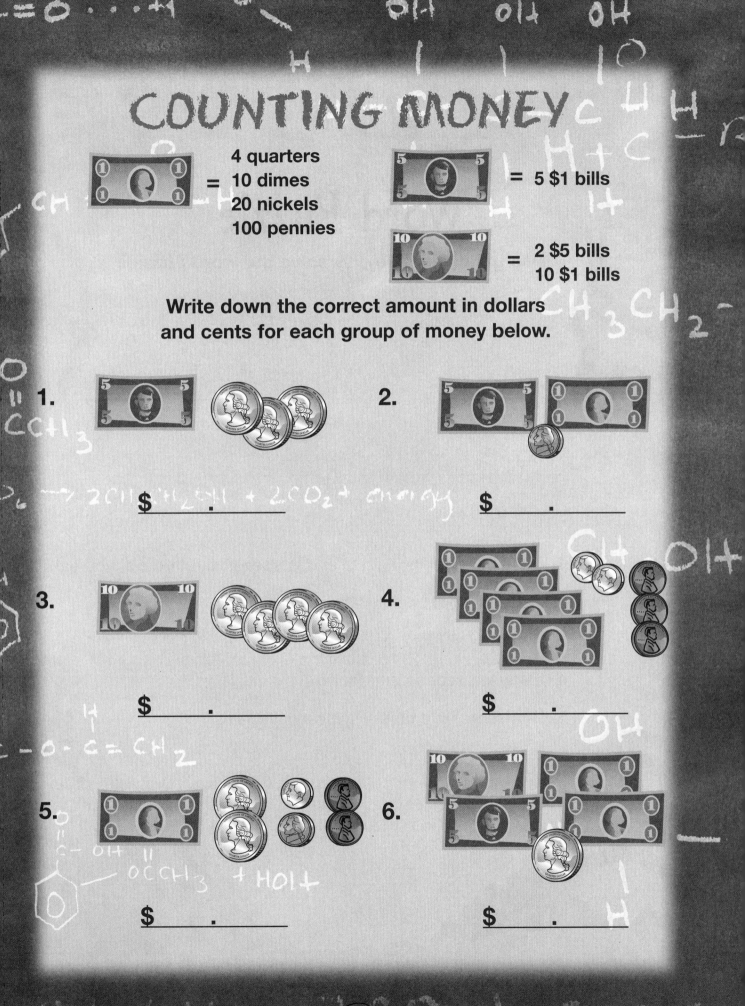

4 quarters
10 dimes = $1 bill
20 nickels
100 pennies

= 5 $1 bills

= 2 $5 bills
  10 $1 bills

Write down the correct amount in dollars and cents for each group of money below.

1. $_____.____

2. $_____.____

3. $_____.____

4. $_____.____

5. $_____.____

6. $_____.____

Word Puzzle

Use the clues below to solve the word puzzle.

_ _ _ _   _ _ _   _ _

_ _ _ _ _   _ _ _ _   _ _

1. First word begins with G and is spelled like the stuff you eat.

2. Second word begins with an L and rhymes with truck.

3. The opposite of out.

4. Between second and fourth.

5. The score on a test—rhymes with maid.

MATH

Follow the patterns and fill in the blanks with the correct numbers. The first one has been done for you.

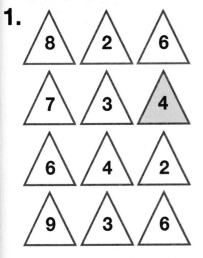

Example:

1.

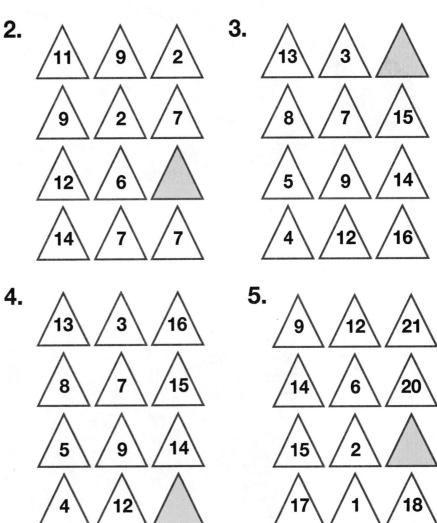

2.

3.

4.

5.

Look at the map on page 158. Describe where you would like to visit in the United States…

_____

_____

_____

_____

CROSSWORD

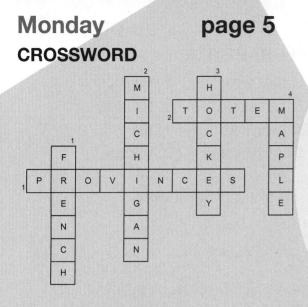

MATH CODED MESSAGES
Answer: CN Tower

MAZE

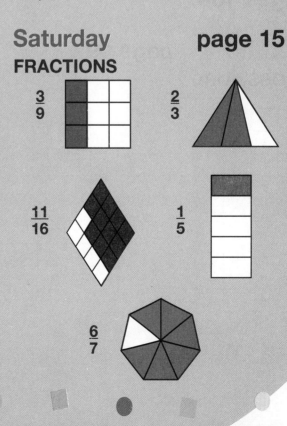

Wednesday   page 8

STORY ACTIVITY 1

1. Luke's older sister.
2. Addison told him to go to the old barn.
3. excited

Wednesday   page 9

STORY ACTIVITY 2

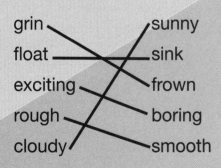

grin — frown
float — sink
exciting — boring
rough — smooth
cloudy — sunny

Friday   page 13

COMPLETE THE STORY
look, country, used, facts, pulled, green, interesting, yelped, symbol, stripes

Saturday   page 15

FRACTIONS

$\frac{3}{9}$ $\frac{2}{3}$

$\frac{11}{16}$ $\frac{1}{5}$

$\frac{6}{7}$

Thursday   page 10

FACT vs. OPINION
1.Fact 2.Opinion 3.Fact
4.Opinion 5.Fact

Week 1
continued

Sunday   page 16

ALPHABETIZE

1. camera
2. passport
3. pictures
4. souvenirs
5. suitcase
6. tourist
7. travel
8. vacation

Sunday   page 17

MATH

1. Answer: 5. Subtract the bottom number from the left number. Subtract the right number from the difference: 8-1-2=5.

2. Answer: 11. Add the three numbers together: 8+1+2.

3. Answer: 7. Add bottom number to left number. Subtract right number from sum: 8+1-2=7.

4. Answer: 5. Add left number to bottom number subtract right number from the difference: 3+3-1=5.

5. Answer: 9. Add the 2 top numbers and subtract the bottom number from the difference: 8+4-3=9.

Week 2
Germany
pages 18-31

Monday   page 19

CROSSWORD

Wednesday   page 22

STORY ACTIVITY 1

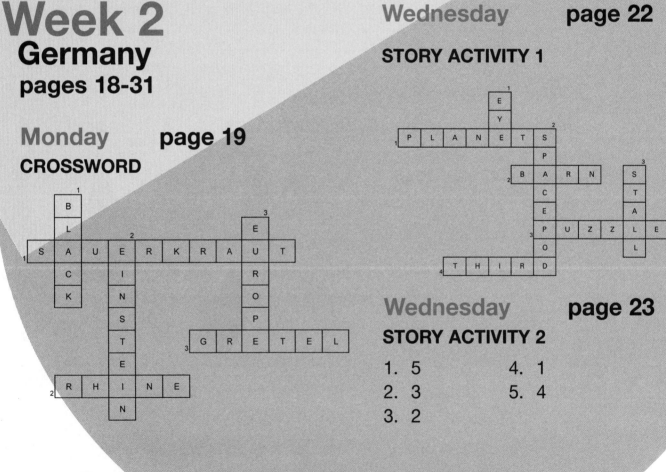

Wednesday   page 23

STORY ACTIVITY 2

1. 5
2. 3
3. 2
4. 1
5. 4

Thursday　　　page 24

SPELLING QUIZ
1. assembly
2. worker
3. machine
4. boxes
5. tools
6. robot
7. computer
8. clipboard

Saturday　　　page 29

ADDITION
1. 323
2. 519
3. 666
4. 903
5. 593
6. 986
7. 899
8. 400
9. 878

Sums > 600? 5
(problems 3, 4, 6, 7, 9)
Sums < 600? 4
(problems 1, 2, 5, 8)
Sums = 600? 0

Friday　　　page 26

MATH CODED MESSAGES
Answer: Bavarian Alps

MAZE

Here's one way!

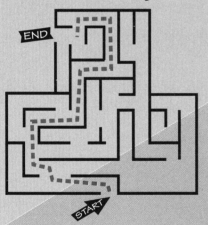

Sunday　　　page 30

PROPER NOUNS
1. **D**ecember, **J**anet, **F**rance
2. **H**alloween, **O**ctober
3. **C**olosseum, **R**ome, **I**taly
4. **J**erry, **T**aj **M**ahal, India

Sunday　　　page 31

MATH
Add the 3 outer numbers and
put the answer in the middle.

1. 17
2. 26
3. 24
4. 15
5. 14

Friday　　　page 27

COMPLETE THE STORY
favorite, pretend, castle,
reading, tales, reached, house,
dessert, oven, laughing

Week 3
Greenland
pages 32–45

Monday   page 33
CROSSWORD

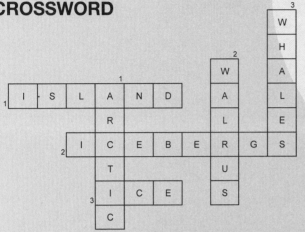

Wednesday   page 36
STORY ACTIVITY 1

1. c
2. d
3. a

Wednesday   page 37
STORY ACTIVITY 2

1. Possible answers include huge and bright.
2. special
3. bright

Thursday   page 38
CONTRACTIONS

1. don't
2. isn't
3. they're
4. I've
5. we've
6. they'll
7. we're
8. you'll

Friday   page 40
MATH CODED MESSAGES
Answer:
Greenlandic and Danish

MAZE
Here's one way!

Friday   page 41
COMPLETE THE STORY
information, report, hummed, largest, summer, sound, called, replied, huge, ice

Saturday   page 43
PERIMETER
Parallelogram: 20 centimeters
Triangle: 12 centimeters
Rectangle: 30 centimeters

Sunday   page 44
LONG VOWELS

note, sheep, kite, cake,
five, wave, cube

Sunday   page 45
MATH

1. Answer: 6. Subtract the bottom number from the left number. Add the difference to the right number: 7-4+3=6

2. Answer: 12. Add the left number to the bottom number. Subtract the right number from their sum: 16+8-12=12

3. Answer: 5. Subtract bottom number from left number. Subtract right number from the difference: 40-20-15=5

4. Answer: 7. Add the left number to the bottom number. Subtract the right number from the sum: 5+9-7=7

5. Answer: 9. Add the left and right numbers. Subtract the bottom number from their sum: 10+8-9=9

Week 4
Ireland
pages 46-59

Monday   page 47
CROSSWORD

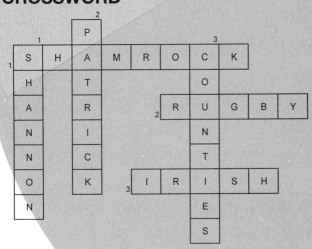

Wednesday   page 50
STORY ACTIVITY 1

My very educated mother just served us nine pizzas.

Mercury, Venus, Earth, Mars, Jupiter, Saturn, Uranus, Neptune, Pluto

Week 4
continued

Thursday   page 52
RHYMING WORDS

1. sheep
2. potatoes
3. fox
4. truck
5. well
6. rock
7. house
8. ball/wall

Friday   page 54
MATH CODED MESSAGES
Answer: Emerald Isle

MAZE

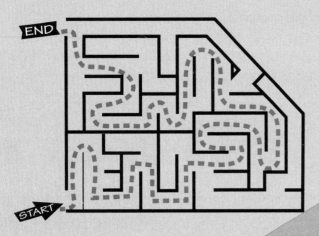

Friday   page 55
COMPLETE THE STORY
photographs, good, legs, people, stand, acrobat, shouted, jump, princess, stories

Saturday   page 57
SUBTRACTION

1. 372
2. 411
3. 670
4. 213
5. 500
6. 500
7. 101
8. 611
9. 551

How many are > than 500? 3
(Numbers 3, 8, 9)
How many are < than 500? 4
(Numbers 1, 2, 4, 7)
How many are = 500? 2
(Numbers 5, 6)

Sunday   page 58
BLENDS
sticker, slip, frog, trick, grab

Sunday   page 59
MATH

1. Answer: 16. Subtract the left number from the right number and add the bottom number to the sum: 12-4+8=16

2. Answer: 7. Add the left number to the right number. Subtract the bottom number from the sum: 8+5-6=7

3. Answer: 4. Add the left number to the right number. Subtract the bottom number from the sum: 13+5-14=4

4. Answer: 11. Add the left number to the bottom number. Subtract the right number from the sum: 14+3-6=11

5. Answer: 9. Add the left number to the bottom number. Subtract the right number from the sum: 9+11-11=9

Monday — page 61

CROSSWORD

```
      1                3
      S                R
 1                     
 C  H  O  P  S  T  I  C  K  S
      O     A          C
      E     C          E
      S     I
            F                4
            I                M
         2                   A
         C  H  E  R  R  Y
```

Wednesday — page 64

STORY ACTIVITY 1

```
N                 S           E
O              U              A
S           P                 R
I        E                    T
D     R                 N     H
D     S                 T     U
A  C  R  A  T  E  R     E  V        S
   O           Y        N  E
   P           R  I  N
E  D           B  U
      I        A  S        C  E  K  U  L
      D     C           R
         G              E
E  T  I  R  O  E  T  E  M        M
               T
```

Wednesday — page 65

STORY ACTIVITY 2

Possible answers include met, or, riot, tire, meet, toe, tore, time, me, it, more, and tie.

Thursday — page 66

POSSESSIVES

1. The (horses) pulled the farmer's wagon.
2. The kid's sandbox had (toys) in it.
3. The girl's kite was very far up in the air.
4. The cat's (kittens) were fluffy and gray.
5. The (boys) went to their friend's house.
6. The (kids) put the school's flag up every morning.

Friday — page 68

MATH CODED MESSAGES

Answer: Todaiji Temple

MAZE

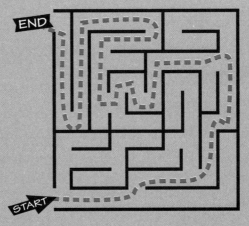

Friday — page 69

COMPLETE THE STORY

mountain, baseball, manufacture, flag, hopped, important, smudge, exclaimed, label, largest

Week 5
continued

Saturday page 71
TELLING TIME

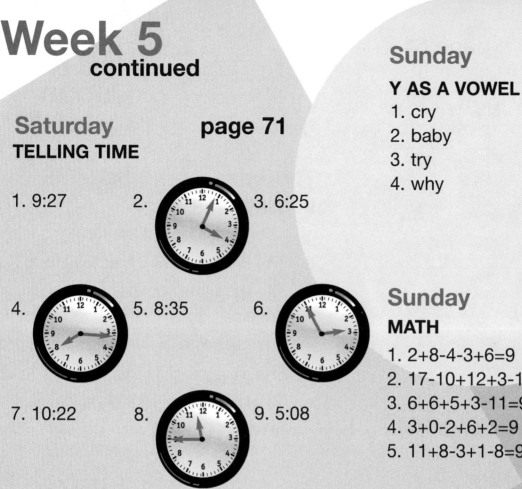

1. 9:27
2.
3. 6:25
4.
5. 8:35
6.
7. 10:22
8.
9. 5:08

Sunday page 72
Y AS A VOWEL
1. cry
2. baby
3. try
4. why

Sunday page 73
MATH
1. 2+8-4-3+6=9
2. 17-10+12+3-13=9
3. 6+6+5+3-11=9
4. 3+0-2+6+2=9
5. 11+8-3+1-8=9

Week 6
Kenya
pages 74-87

Monday page 75
CROSSWORD

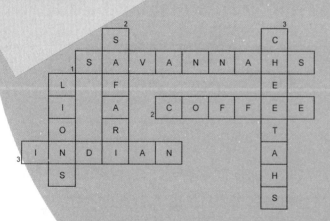

Wednesday page 78
STORY ACTIVITY 1
1. Luke can't see anything but clouds.
2. It is closer to Earth's size than the other planets.
3. Seven miles high.
4. Flat in some parts, but has mountains, volcanoes, and craters in others.

Wednesday page 79
STORY ACTIVITY 2
1. Venus and a greenhouse.

Thursday page 80

HOMONYMS

1. sun
2. four
3. weather
4. bare
5. grown
6. pair

Saturday page 85

MATH PUZZLE
Answer:
ADDISON AND D.I.D.G.E.T.

Friday page 82

MATH CODED MESSAGES
Answer: Swahili and English

MAZE

Sunday page 86

SOFT C VS. HARD C

1. cat-hard
2. candy-hard
3. celery-soft
4. city-soft
5. crib-hard
6. cider-soft

Friday page 83

COMPLETE THE STORY
complained, listen, treasures, sitting, found, animals, language, wondered, picture, zoo

Sunday page 87

MATH

1. 5+3+1+9-4=14
2. 20+10+4-20+or-0=14
3. 17+11-8-18+12=14
4. 8+10-6+10-8=14
5. 14+3-2-5+4=14

Week 7
Mexico
pages 88-101

Wednesday page 92

STORY ACTIVITY 1

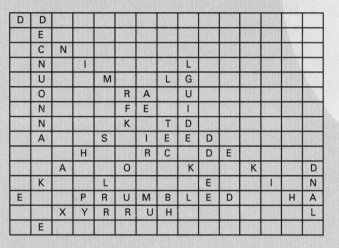

Wednesday page 93

STORY ACTIVITY 2

Mercury:
  flat in places
  craters
  800°F (427°C)
  3 times closer to the sun than
  Earth is

Venus:
  Earth's twin
  half the planet is flat
  craters, mountains, and volcanoes
  hotter than Mercury

Mars:
  reddish-orange dirt
  craters

CROSSWORD

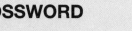

Thursday page 94
CORRECT THE SENTENCES

1. Mexico is surrounded by the Pacific Ocean and the Gulf of Mexico.
2. Have you ever seen a bullfighter?
3. Chili peppers are used in Mexican dishes.
4. There are many beautiful beaches in Mexico! (! or . after Mexico are both correct.)

Friday page 96
MATH CODED MESSAGES
Answer: Chihuahua

MAZE

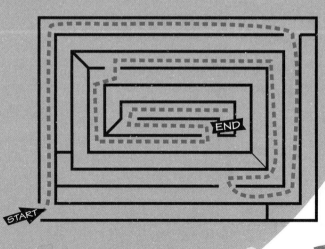

Friday — page 97

COMPLETE THE STORY

attic, large, lifted, papier-mâché, shaped, tail, feathers, grabbed, piñata, breaks

Saturday — page 99

COUNTING MONEY

1. one quarter
2. fifteen pennies
3. zero quarters
4. two dimes

Sunday — page 100

ADVERBS

1. c
2. d
3. a
4. b

Sunday — page 101

MATH

1. 4+3+4+6-9=8
2. 6+5-10+12-5=8
3. 17-9-8+10-2=8
4. 5-1+8+3-7=8
5. 19+2-7-7+1=8

Week 8
Norway
pages 102-115

Monday — page 103

CROSSWORD

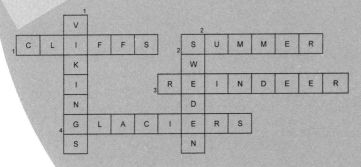

Wednesday — page 106

STORY ACTIVITY 1

1. All Aboard the Space Pod
2. inside the Space Pod
3. Addison, Luke, D.I.D.G.E.T.
4. Possible answer: Luke wants to find Martian water. He will find a sample of Martian water to bring back to Earth.
5. Possible answer: Addison, Luke, and D.I.D.G.E.T. will return to Earth with information about all of the planets.

Week 8
continued

Wednesday page 107

STORY ACTIVITY 2

1. 1
2. 3
3. 2
4. 5
5. 4

Thursday page 108

PAST TENSE VERBS

1. The bear floated down the river.
2. The Vikings waved at everyone.
3. The fish jumped out of the water.
4. The man skied down the mountain.
5. The boats sailed in the river.

Friday page 110

MATH CODED MESSAGES
Answer: Arctic Circle

MAZE

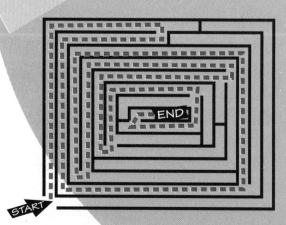

Friday page 111

COMPLETE THE STORY
game, dragons, threw, Vikings, noises, long, tape, spoon, map, jagged

Saturday page 113

HELP ADDISON FIND D.I.D.G.E.T.

20	9	30	40	50	65	90	100	35	10
5	5	10	15	30	45	60	75	80	85
70	25	50	20	15	30	25	45	25	30
65	50	30	25	45	70	45	50	20	35
60	55	35	65	55	60	65	55	15	5
70	50	40	45	50	40	70	60	10	100
80	35	30	60	65	70	75	80	80	95
75	40	45	70	55	65	75	85	90	70
85	50	35	80	60	50	70	80	95	80
95	65	25	10	20	55	65	90	100	50

Sunday page 114

PARTS OF SPEECH

1. b
2. e
3. f
4. a
5. d
6. c

Sunday page 115

MATH

1. 4+3-4+6-9=0
2. 12-2+10-5-15=0
3. 5+7+7-12-7=0
4. 17-12+3+2-10=0
5. 9+13+3-20-5=0

Monday   page 117
CROSSWORD

```
              3
              P         4
      2       I         A
      I   2   G R A N D  N
  1   N   G R A N D      D
  L   C                  E
  L   A                  S
1 A M A Z O N
  M   S         H
  A             A
```

Thursday   page 122
ANTONYMS, SYNONYMS, AND HOMONYMS

1. synonym
2. homonym
3. antonym

4. antonym
5. synonym
6. homonym

Wednesday   page 120

STORY ACTIVITY 1

1. He ran to get on the Space Pod before it took off without him.
2. He dropped the ice sample from Mars.
3. She was concerned.

Friday   page 124
MATH CODED MESSAGES
Answer: Huascarán

MAZE

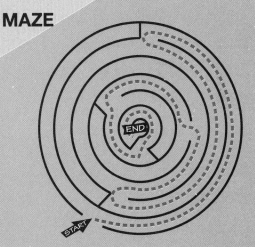

Wednesday   page 121

STORY ACTIVITY 2

1. whispered
2. hopped
3. strolled
4. dashed

Friday   page 125
COMPLETE THE STORY
stared, looked, humming, spooky, believed, helping, mountains, mummies, preserved, learn

Week 9
continued

Saturday   page 127

PLACE VALUES

1. 4,474   **5.** 4,263

2.

1000s	100s	10s	1s
///	/////	////	/////////

6.

1000s	100s	10s	1s
/////	///	///////	//

3. 6,555   **7.** 8,916

4.

1000s	100s	10s	1s
//	////	///	/////

8.

1000s	100s	10s	1s
////	/////	///	/////

Sunday   page 129

SOLAR SYSTEM CROSSWORD

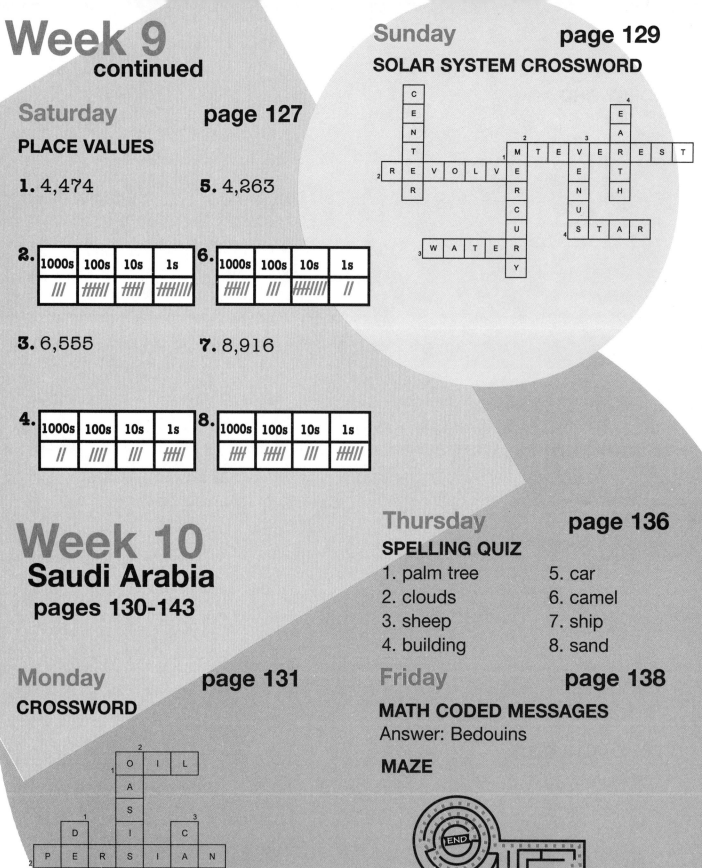

Across: 2. REVOLVE 1. MT EVEREST 3. WATER 4. STAR
Down: CENTR MERCURY TEETH EARTH STAR

Week 10
Saudi Arabia
pages 130-143

Monday   page 131

CROSSWORD

Across: 1. OIL 2. PERSIAN 3. ASIA
Down: OASIS DISI DESERT CAMEL

Thursday   page 136

SPELLING QUIZ

1. palm tree
2. clouds
3. sheep
4. building

5. car
6. camel
7. ship
8. sand

Friday   page 138

MATH CODED MESSAGES
Answer: Bedouins

MAZE

Friday page 139

COMPLETE THE STORY

attic, camel, spit, carry, desert, feet, sand, many, eyelashes, like

Saturday page 141

MULTIPLICATION

1. 1x10=10
2. 1x1=1
3. 1x9=9
4. 1x7=7
5. 1x8=8
6. 1x14=14
7. 1x99=99
8. 1x17=17
9. 1x24=24

Sunday page 143

SOLAR SYSTEM CROSSWORD

Monday page 145

CROSSWORD

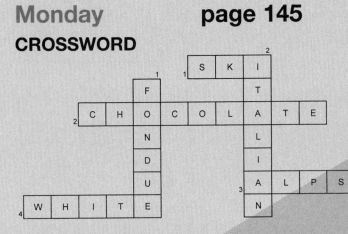

Wednesday page 149

STORY ACTIVITY 2

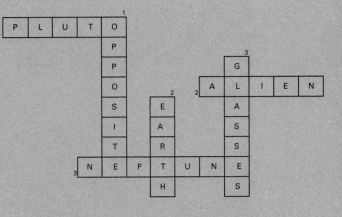

Wednesday page 148

STORY ACTIVITY 1

Addison: Possible answers: smart, inventor, in third grade, Luke's sister, a leader

Luke: Possible answers: younger brother of Addison, adventurous, admires his sister, curious

D.I.D.G.E.T.: Possible answers: computer invented by Addison, small as a book, knows everything, likes to share his facts

Thursday page 150

SILENT LETTERS

1. k
2. w
3. c
4. b
5. w
6. gh
7. h
8. gh

Friday — page 152

MATH CODED MESSAGES
Answer: Neuchatal

MAZE

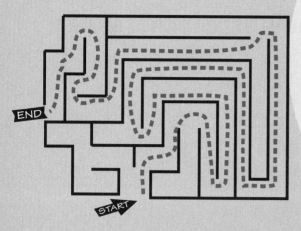

Friday — page 153

COMPLETE THE STORY
reading, blue, hiking, trail, page, picture, grass, wobbly, turned, speaking

Saturday — page 155

MULTIPLICATION
1. 1x2=2
2. 5x2=10
3. 3x2=6
4. 7x2=14
5. 10x2=20
6. 8x2=16
7. 6x2=12
8. 2x2=4
9. 9x2=18

Sunday — page 157

SOLAR SYSTEM CROSSWORD

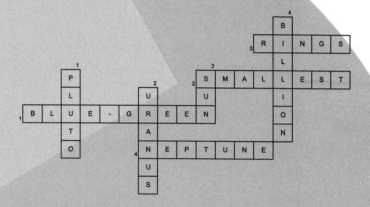

Monday — page 159

CROSSWORD

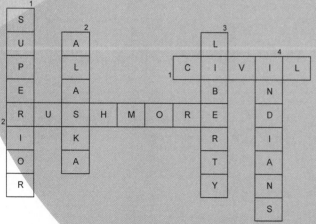

Week 12
United States
pages 158-171

Wednesday — page 162

STORY ACTIVITY 1
1. Mars
2. Jupiter, Saturn, Uranus, and Neptune
3. to protect the pod from the heat
4. Earth
5. He shares facts and other important information.

Wednesday page 163

STORY ACTIVITY 2

1. 3
2. 1
3. 5
4. 6
5. 4
6. 2

Thursday page 164

FIVE SENSES

1. touch
2. taste
3. hearing
4. smell
5. sight

Friday page 166

MATH CODED MESSAGES

Answer: Ellis Island

MAZE

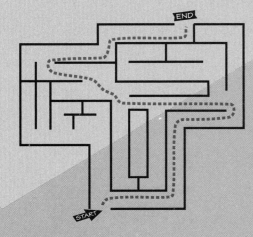

Friday page 167

COMPLETE THE STORY

flag, box, clues, bored, disagreed, foods, cheese, plain, flashed, beeped

Saturday page 169

COUNTING MONEY

1. $5.75
2. $6.05
3. $11.00
4. $4.23
5. $1.67
6. $17.25

Sunday page 170

WORD PUZZLE

1. Good 2. Luck 3. In
4. Third 5. Grade
Answer: Good Luck In
        Third Grade

Sunday page 171

MATH

1. 7-3=4
2. 12-6=6
3. 13+3=16
4. 4+12=16
5. 15+2=17

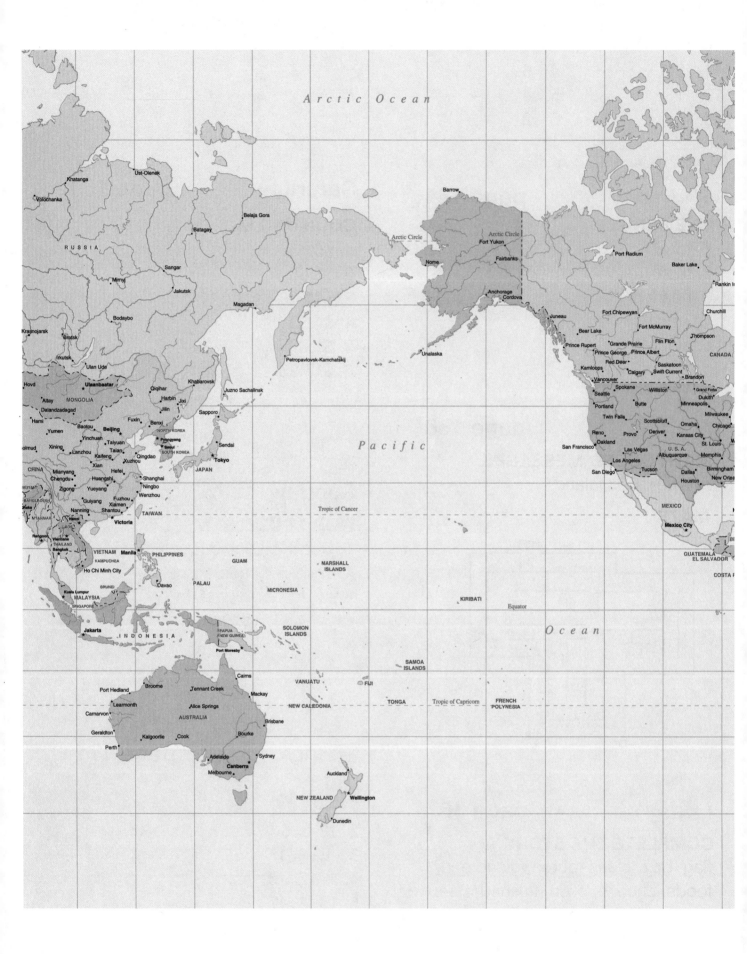

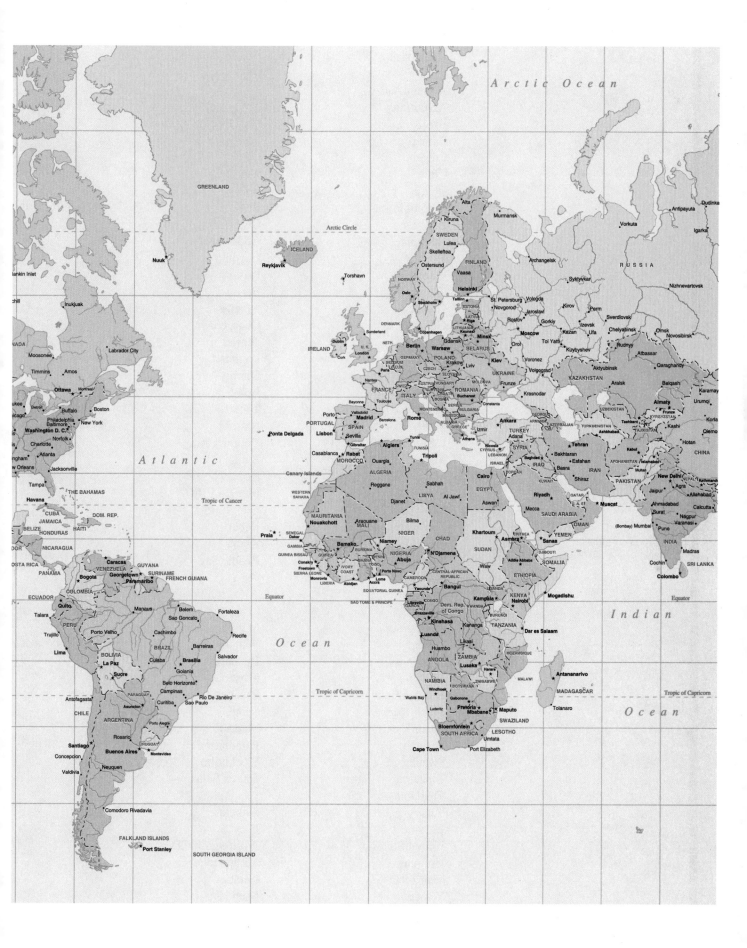

World Geography

Countries	Capitals
Afghanistan	Kabul
Argentina	Buenos Aires
Brazil	Brasília
Cameroon	Yaoundé
Canada	Ottawa
Chile	Santiago
China	Beijing
Colombia	Bogotá
Ecuador	Quito
Ethiopia	Addis Ababa
Finland	Helsinki
France	Paris
Germany	Berlin
Greece	Athens
Guyana	Georgetown
Iran	Tehran
Iraq	Baghdad
Ireland	Dublin
Italy	Rome
Japan	Tokyo
Kenya	Nairobi
Libya	Tripoli
Mali	Bamako
Mauritania	Nouakchott
Mexico	Mexico City
Mongolia	Ulan Bator
Morocco	Rabat
Nigeria	Abuja
North Korea	Pyongyang
Norway	Oslo
Paraguay	Asunción
Peru	Lima
Philippines	Manila
Poland	Warsaw
Romania	Bucharest
Russia	Moscow
Saudi Arabia	Riyadh
South Korea	Seoul
Spain	Madrid
Surinam	Paramaribo
Sweden	Stockholm
Tanzania	Dar es Salaam
Thailand	Bangkok
Turkey	Ankara
Ukraine	Kiev
United States	Washington, D.C.
Uruguay	Montevideo
Venezuela	Caracas
Yemen	Sana
Zimbabwe	Harare